The Essential Consumer's Guide to CAR RE[...]
Simple and Straightforward Information w[...]
Step-by-Step Instructions and Diagrams

The Car Repair Book

JACK GILLIS

with TOM KELLY and

Seth Krevat   Amy Burch
Alisa Feingold   Cheryl Denenberg

Julie Beth Wright

Illustrations by Al Kettler

HarperPerennial
A Division of HarperCollins*Publishers*

Publisher's Note

Every reasonable effort has been made to ensure the accuracy and reliability of the information, instructions and directions contained in this book. However, success and safety in making automotive repairs depends on individual accuracy, care, caution, judgment and skill. The publisher and the author specifically disclaim any personal liability for misinterpretation of directions, human error, typographical mistakes or other loss or risk incurred as a consequence of the advice or information presented in this book.

Also by Jack Gillis

The Car Book
The Used Car Book
The Childwise Catalog (coauthor)
How to Make Your Car Last Almost Forever
The Armchair Mechanic (coauthor)
How to Fly (coauthor)
The Bank Book (editor)
The Product Safety Book (editor)
The Truck, Van, and 4x4 Book

Library of Congress Cataloging-in-Publication Data

Gillis, Jack.
    The car repair book : the essential consumer's guide to car repair
    / Jack Gillis.
        p.   cm.
    ISBN 0-06-271522-4 — ISBN 0-06-273062-2 (pbk.)
    1. Automobiles—Maintenance and repair—Amateurs' manuals.
I. Title.
TL152.G5193 1991
629.28'722—dc20   89-46093

91 92 93 94 95 CK 10 9 8 7 6 5 4 3 2 1
91 92 93 94 95 CK 10 9 8 7 6 5 4 3 2 1 (pbk.)

Contents

Acknowledgements

The many names on the title page of this book attest to the fact that it was truly a team effort. In addition to the wise and thoughtful repair advice from Tom Kelly, "our master mechanic", this book was only possible thanks to the many, many hours of research, writing, and organizational effort put in by Amy Burch, Cheryl Denenberg, Seth Krevat, and Julie Beth Wright. The book was artfully prepared, using Pagemaker, by Alisa Feingold, who gracefully composed our words. Adding clarity to those words were the excellent line drawings of illustrator Al Kettler. Rounding out the team were graphic artists Susan Cole and Ben Crenshaw, computer wiz and artist Donna Whitlow, and Mark Jacobsohn and Carol Nansel. Very special thanks go to Karen Fierst who kept everything going in the meantime and came in at the end to help us meet the deadline and superagent Stuart Krichevsky for convincing me that we could, in fact, do it.

Finally, to Marilyn, Katie, John and Brian...thanks for waiting, I'm back!

J.G.

As always,

For Marilyn,
Katie, John, and Brian

Introduction

Although your car's inner workings may seem intimidating, there's really no secret to taking care of and repairing your car. The key is in knowing what you should and shouldn't do, which is what *The Car Repair Book* is all about.

Knowing the basics of car repair will not only save you money, it will also make you a better buyer when it comes to getting the repairs done that you can't do yourself.

The simple fact is, you do not have to be an engineer, a trained mechanic, or even a car expert to perform basic maintenance and repairs on your car. The level of complexity that you're willing to try is up to you. Some people choose to do most of the work themselves, and others will never even open the glove box! Like most of us, you probably fall somewhere in between.

Even if you've never considered opening the hood, understanding what it takes to keep a car in good shape, including what kinds of fuel to use, what kinds of service are needed, how to recognize dangerous symptoms while in the driver's seat, and a range of reasonable prices for various kinds of repair, can be very helpful. If you feel intimidated by the apparent complexity of an automobile, taking it one step at a time will increase your confidence and, as a result, reduce the costs and hassles of car ownership. *The Car Repair Book* can be your starting point!

We understand that "easy" is a relative word. While straightening and re-painting a crumpled fender may be simple for an experienced body repair technician, most of us would not even know where to begin. Well, this is the book for "most" of us.

We designed *The Car Repair Book* so you can try as much--or as little--as you choose. You can learn to check the level of your engine oil without knowing anything about the phenomena of "quench" or "squish." If you don't want to know how to check your oil, you will at least find out how often to have it checked to avoid the risk of ruining your engine.

The Car Repair Book will give you a basic understanding of how your car works, teach you the key preventative maintenance checks, and help you find out what your car is trying to tell you when it clanks, gurgles, or squeals.

Chapter One will breeze you through the basic operation of your car--*How It Works* and what can go wrong. You'll learn that the coolant in your radiator is not the only way your engine keeps from overheating--your engine oil and fan also play an important role. In Chapter Two, we'll acquaint you with the basic *Tools*--just what you need to do basic repairs. Chapter Three tells you what you need to know to *Keep it Going* for years to come. We also offer tips on breaking in your new car, getting through the winter, and saving gas.

In Chapter Four, we take you *Under the Hood*. After explaining what's what, you'll find out how to do many of the checks and simple repairs to some of those complicated looking parts.

Chapter Five is your guide to what's *Under Your Car* and what you can actually do to keep it in shape. Next we'll give you the run down on the *Electrical System*--how to keep it running and what to do when it doesn't. In Chapter Seven we'll look at what makes your engine go--*The Fuel System*--including some tips on choosing the right gas. A key element in the value of your car is how it looks. Chapters Eight and Nine will help you keep it shiny and fix what's broken--inside and out.

How many times have you heard a strange rumble or smelled something funny? What does it really mean when one of your dash lights goes on? Knowing what a particular symptom indicates could mean the difference between an inexpensive repair and a major overhaul. Chapter Ten explains how to *Troubleshoot* like the pros-- what those smells and noises may mean and how best to handle them.

Because this is a book for beginners, there's a lot that you *won't* be doing to your car. In Chapter Eleven, we'll teach you how to talk to *Your Mechanic* and save money in the process. Finally, if you want *More Information,* you'll find some sources listed in Chapter Twelve.

That's what this book is all about--a simple, straightforward guide to repairing one of the most complex products you will ever own.

You don't have to read the entire book before you begin, but we've worked hard to keep the information simple enough so it wouldn't be too difficult to do so. We've also tried to keep each repair on a page, so you won't have to fumble around finding the rest of the repair.

How We Rate the Repairs: We place each repair in the book in one of three categories: *Basic, Beyond Basic,* and *Adventuresome.*

If you can pick up this book and read it, you can do the repairs we've listed as *Basic.* A *Basic* repair can usually be accomplished in a short period of time with fairly simple tools. *Beyond Basic* repairs require a little

more effort, time, and tools. The final category, *Adventuresome*, may seem a little intimidating. To do these repairs you might have to consult what is called a shop manual for the car. The shop manual is a dense volume that covers most every repair to your make and model. Many libraries and parts stores have shop manuals.

Safety First: Fixing a car poses few safety hazards if you take the proper precautions. Most accidents and injuries can be prevented if you follow generally accepted safety advice. When reading the repairs in this book, you will notice safety tips that alert you to areas posing possible problems--please consider them.

Getting Started: The key to success is to pick the *Basic* repairs first. Even performing the simplest tasks will get you better acquainted with your car. You will often find that a part from one section of the car may have similar attachments (such as electrical wires or clamps) to another part. The more you work on your car, the more *Adventuresome* you are likely to become in tackling more difficult repairs.

Most of us are our own worst enemy when it comes to do-it-yourself car repairs.

Try not to be intimidated. Remember, repairing a car is not brain surgery. If a step by step process is followed, most repairs are as simple as following the directions for a recipe in a cookbook. We recommend reading through the repair before making the decision to do it. If possible, try to read it while looking at your car.

As you begin, remember that your not alone as a beginner. Thousands of service stations have disappeared in recent years due to the emergence of self-serve stations. This change means that there are fewer places available to work on your car. As a result, there are many more do-it-yourselfers today than ever. Today, more than 60 percent of new air and oil filters, 50 percent of new batteries, and 40 percent of all new shock absorbers are replaced by do-it-yourselfers.

Can you save significant amounts of money doing your own service on a car? Yes. To replace a headlight can cost $35, an alternator, $150. Doing it yourself can more than cut those costs in half, and you'll hardly even get your fingers dirty.

As you begin, remember, you can do it! And not only that, you'll feel great when you're done--and so will your car.

1

There is no question that a car can be intimidating. In fact, the idea of actually fixing one yourself may seem impossible. While cars have become increasingly intricate, there are still many simple money saving repairs that any of us can do. The more you understand how your car works, the better you'll be able to get the right repairs done, even if you don't do them yourself.

This chapter is the "big picture," an overview of your car and how it works. Even if you never do a repair in your life, just by reading the next few pages you will dramatically increase your ability to get the right repairs done at a reasonable price. The fact of the matter is, while the various components that make up a car have become quite complex, the basic operation (how it works) has changed little since the Model T. So don't be daunted by the fact that you may not know everything about your car. In fact, nobody does!

In This Chapter...
How It Works
The Internal Combustion Engine
The Systems

Here's How It Works

The reason a modern automobile seems complex is that it *is* complex. An incredible number of parts--some estimates are as high as 10,000--work together to make the car move forward when you step on the gas. Fortunately, you don't need to understand all of your car's parts. For many repairs, all you need is some basic information about the parts involved.

As a single machine, every automobile is made up of three kinds of systems. It doesn't matter whether it's a Lamborghini Countach or a Ford Model T, all cars have the same three systems: mechanical, electrical, and fuel.

Within each of these systems there are sub-systems, which are also often referred to as systems. The ignition system is part of the electrical system, and the cooling system is part of the mechanical system. Some sub-systems are parts of two or more kinds of basic systems. For example, the emission control system is a single sub-system that is partly mechanical, partly electrical, and partly fuel.

Each sub-system is composed of a varying number of assemblies. Depending on year, make, model, and optional equipment, the number of possible assemblies is very large. Here are a few examples. A distributor is an assembly that is part of the ignition system, which is part of the electrical system. An alternator is part of the charging system, which is also part of the electrical system. A shock absorber is part of the suspension system, which is one of the mechanical systems. Your transmission, automatic or manual, is an assembly. So is your engine. And so on.

Finally, each assembly is made up of individual parts. A rotor for example, is part of the distributor assembly. Another kind of rotor, sometimes also called a disc, is part of the brake assembly on a vehicle equipped with disc brakes. A pulley is the part of your alternator that enables a belt to connect the alternator to the engine, so that the alternator can convert mechanical engine power to electricity. A wiper blade insert is part of your windshield wiper assembly.

One part of many assemblies in virtually every make and model car is known as a lockwasher. This simple mechanical device prevents a nut or bolt from coming loose as the result of vibration. Two basic types, the split ring lockwasher and the internal star lockwasher, are most commonly used on automobiles. When compressed by tightening the nut or bolt, the lockwasher produces an extraordinary amount of friction, which keeps the connection tight.

There. You now know how and why the lockwasher works. You thoroughly understand one indispensable part of a car.

There is no doubt that the list of parts in your car is long. In fact, dealerships and automotive parts warehouses used to have a set of books, called the "Weatherly Index," that listed every part of every assembly of every system of every car. A complete set, incorporating past and current books, would fill all the shelves in a fair-sized room. Today, this detailed information is in computer memory. Manufacturers, distributors, and retailers can all access databases when a customer orders a part.

The good news about knowing that your car has so many parts is that many, many of them are easy to repair.

The Internal Combustion Engine

In addition to understanding that the car is made up of systems, it helps to understand how these systems work together. In other words, here's what happens when you turn your key.

When you turn the key to start your car, two things happen: First, an electric motor (the starter) cranks the engine, moving the pistons inside the cylinders, and second, electricity is sent to the spark plugs.

The motion of the pistons sucks a mixture of air and gasoline into the cylinders, and the spark plugs ignite the mixture with a spark. The resulting combustion drives the piston downward. It is this expansion, taking place milliseconds apart in each cylinder in the engine, that generates energy to keep the car running.

Most cars use an internal combustion engine, which has at its heart the cylinders that contain the pistons. The combustion process takes place in four steps:

1. Intake: As the piston moves down, the air/fuel mixture is drawn into the cylinder through a special valve.

2. Compression: As the piston moves back up, the air/fuel intake valve closes, and the mixture compresses against the cylinder's top.

3. Power: The instant the piston reaches the top of its stroke, a spark from the spark plug ignites the mixture, causing a mini-explosion, called combustion, which drives the piston back down and provides energy to the car.

4. Exhaust: The piston then moves back up, forcing the residue from the combustion out a release valve. The burned gases exit the car via the exhaust pipe and muffler. The process then repeats itself.

Sometimes, a weak spark plug will fail to ignite the fuel. This can be the cause of popping noises (backfiring) that you occasionally hear from the tailpipe. The unignited air/fuel mixture ignites in your exhaust system.

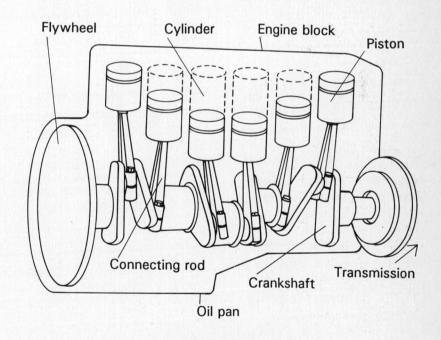

Internal Combustion Engine

The Systems

Now that you have a basic idea of how the engine works, here is a quick review of the rest of the systems that make it go.

The **suspension system** on the car keeps the passengers and the body of the car from feeling the many bumps and dips of the road. It also limits the swaying back and forth when turning and the dipping up and down when accelerating and braking. The front wheels of most cars are independently supported so that a bump on one side will not affect the other, and some high performance and luxury cars also have independent rear suspension.

The **braking system** uses the mechanical advantage of hydraulic pressure to allow the driver to stop the massive weight of an automobile with a fair amount of ease. With this system, a relatively light touch of the foot can stop your car, even when it is traveling at 55 mph.

The steering system controls the wheels in order to direct the car. Many cars now use a booster in power steering that makes steering easier.

In a rear drive automobile, the **drive line** is the device that transmits power from the engine assembly to the rear axle. It is centered under the car at the rear of the transmission, and it extends to the rear wheels. Connecting the drive line to the rear wheels is the differential. This clever device allows the outside wheels to turn faster than the inside wheels when turning a corner.

In front drive cars, the **drive line** is much shorter and somewhat more complex. A compact device known as the transaxle replaces the transmission, differential, and rear axle. This assembly accepts power from the engine and performs all of the functions of the transmission in delivering power to both front wheels.

The **oil system** lubricates the engine, helping to minimize friction and to keep the engine cool. It circulates oil through the engine block, and it keeps the engine clean and functioning.

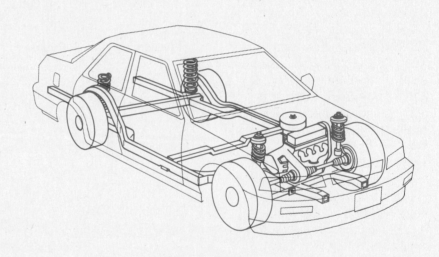

Suspension System

The **exhaust system** transmits the burned gases produced by the engine to a safe location away from the driver. This location is usually at the rear of the car, but in many large trucks the exhaust system is installed vertically, discharging the gases near the top of the cab.

The alternator in an automobile's **charging system** changes mechanical energy (the rotation of the engine) into electrical energy. As its name suggests, the alternator produces AC (alternating current) similar to household electrical current. The alternator is also used to charge the battery.

Up until about 20 years ago, generators served the same purpose. The generator is a DC (direct current) device, which produces energy similar to a battery, with a single positive and a single negative pole. Alternators weigh less than a generator of similar output and are more efficient, creating more electricity with less drain on the engine.

The **electrical system** is what originally starts the car and keeps it running. It provides energy to the pistons to start get them moving and then continuously supplies energy to the spark plugs to keep the process going.

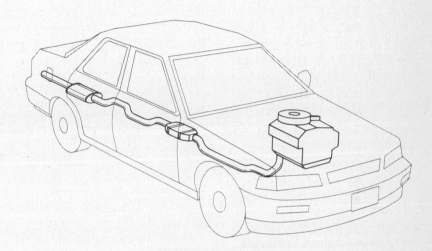

The Exhaust System

The Electrical System

The **cooling system** keeps the heat that an automobile engine produces under control. In order to keep the engine cool, the engine block is surrounded by a blanket of flowing water and coolant which draws the heat away from the engine and into the radiator. Air blows across the radiator to cool the hot water before it returns to the engine.

The **fuel system** supplies the engine with the gasoline required for combustion. The fuel tank stores the gas and the fuel pump pumps the gas from the tank to the engine. The fuel is filtered, and then it is mixed with air in a specific proportion for combustion.

So now you know how your car works. In addition to more detailed descriptions of these and other systems, this book will provide information about how each of the systems in your car interacts with the others. Having a clearer idea of how your car functions will enable you to diagnose a problem and will make you a more confident do-it-yourselfer.

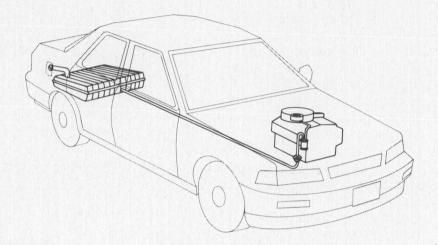

The Fuel System

2

When it comes to doing it yourself, the best rule is to acquire tools gradually. In fact, most tools will pay for themselves if you only buy what you need for a specific job. And over time, as you collect various tools from the different jobs, you'll find that the extent of your tool box reflects your growing knowledge of car repair.

In This Chapter...

Your Tool Box	Emergencies
Buying Car Parts	Safety

Your Toolbox

Often the complexity of the tool has nothing to do with the complexity of the job. Some of the simplest jobs, such as tightening a bolt properly, require an advanced tool, such as a click-type torque wrench. Some of the most advanced jobs, such as adjusting intake and exhaust valves, can be done with tools as a wrench.

For the most frequently used tools, such as wrenches, pliers, and screwdrivers, look for quality, which usually means paying more. Tools used more infrequently, such as a spark plug boot puller or Torx driver, can be of lower quality.

The best criterion for selecting a good quality tool is that it has a lifetime guarantee against breakage or failure. Sears, for example, will replace at no charge a 20-year old, well-used, discolored Craftsman brand wrench that was somehow broken. Other high quality brands include Proto, (an acronym for pro-fessional tools,) S-K, Mac, and Snap-On. Makita is the benchmark of quality for hand-held small power tools.

Craftsman tools, obviously, are sold through Sears stores. The Proto brand is marketed through specialty tool shops, and S-K is found at parts stores that deal in quality merchandise. Mac and Snap-On are competitors, each distributed through "Wagon Jobbers." These are independent dealers who regularly call on professional mechanics. They carry their merchandise in an enclosed van, and their tools are available for immediate sale to anyone. The trick is to ask your regular mechanic when the Snap-On man visits, or check the Yellow Pages for a Snap-On regional distributor.

Even if you decide not to do much repair work yourself, a small investment in some basic tools could mean the difference between waiting by a deserted road for assistance that may be hours in coming and a quick repair that could get you right back on the road. Even if you cannot make the repair yourself, a passenger or passerby may be able to assist you if you have the basic tools and spare parts that are needed.

You'll also need a toolbox to keep all of your supplies together. Toolboxes range from the simplest plastic trays, similar to trays for garden tools, all the way up to huge, movable chests with multiple drawers, used by professional mechanics. It is sensible for a "Basic" do-it-yourselfer to begin with a simple, inexpensive toolbox from a hardware store.

As the number of tools increases, an additional toolbox can be bought, and the tools divided, either by type of tool or by frequency of use. Mechanics with many years experience often have a collection of fifteen or twenty toolboxes, which usually includes the first toolbox they ever owned.

The right tool can make a difficult job easy and the wrong one can make an easy job hard. This section provides some general advice on tools that will come in handy for repair jobs. How many tools you have is a function of how much you feel comfortable doing.

For basic pliers we suggest the adjustable joint variety. Noticeably longer than common pliers, their jaws are tilted about thirty degrees away from the handles, and a long groove on one side allows them to be adjusted from a small to a large opening. Because of their design, adjustable joint pliers allow enormous amounts of leverage on a great variety of work, without marring the surface of the work.

Another pair of pliers worth owning are snipe nose pliers. These look like ordinary needle nose pliers except that they are drastically slimmed down toward the tip. Unfortunately, because they are both strong and narrow, snipe nose pliers are difficult and expensive to manufacture. Snipe nose pliers have a number of uses, including positioning tiny parts and pulling broken keys out of locks.

Your tool box should also contain clamping pliers and an adjustable wrench. The clamping pliers have jaws that can wrap around objects and seize them in an adjustable vise grip. The adjustable wrench has two crescent-shaped jaws, one of which is slid along the other by an adjustable knob.

Something you will often find on newer cars is a Torx head screw. The shape of the head is patented, and it requires a patented screw driver. Car makers are using these screws on headlights, lens covers, dashboards, interior trim of all kinds, and parts of the engine. You will need a Torx head screwdriver to work with these Torx screws. There is a different driver for each size and each grips and holds the screw in any position, including straight down. It won't let go until you want it to.

If you get serious about do-it-yourself work, consider buying a volt-ohm-milliammeter, or multi-meter. It can help you solve dozens of problems around your car, from checking the resistance of spark plug wires to testing light bulbs. Don't be put off because a multi-meter looks complicated at first glance. You can learn to use the instrument one function at a time. If you buy a good meter, it will come with a complete instruction book.

Keeping Clean

Many solvents, and even motor oil, can enter your body through your skin. Disposable latex gloves offer your skin and fingernails protection from dirt, oil, and grease although not from scratches. They're much easier to put on if you first put talcum powder on your hands.

There are also hand creams that you apply before working that make it easy to clean your hands. These creams are not soluble in grease, and therefore do not allow it to adhere to your skin. They are soluble in water, and wash off freely. You'll find this product at most auto parts stores.

Although, there are thousands of tools that can be used for work on your car, a few basic, good choices will enable you to do a variety of maintenance and repair without spending a lot of money. Listed below are the tools that you will need for most of the repairs in this book and safety items that will leave you prepared in case of an emergency.

Torx Screw

A Torx Screw is one which must be removed or installed with a Torx bit. The shape is patented, and Torx is a registered trademark. Torx bits, found on Torx screwdrivers and as separate bits for socket sets, have six grooves which fit by friction into the head of a Torx screw. The bit holds firmly to the screw in any position, but it also releases virtually without effort.

Your Toolbox

Screwdrivers

Large flat head (10" to 15")
Small flat head
Small Phillips head
Medium Phillips head
Torx head

Wrenches

Medium adjustable
Crescent wrench
Socket set
Tubing wrench
Spark plug socket

Pliers

Regular pliers
Clamping pliers
Snipe nose pliers

Other Items

Wire cutter
Rubber hammer
Pry bar (15" to 18")
Clamp or mechanic's light
Jack stands
Sharp knife
Rags
Electrical tape
Duct tape

Spare Parts

Fan or alternator belt(s)
Spark plugs
Cooling hoses
Hose clamps
Transmission fluid
Motor oil
Brake fluid

Secrets from the Pros

Anti-Seize Compound

Any time one metal is threaded into another and tightened, the softer metal tends to weld itself to the harder one. For example, a steel spark plug may weld into an aluminum cylinder head. Even hardened steel bolts applied into cast iron, such as cylinder head mounting bolts, can weld themselves together when subjected to sufficient torque and temperature changes over time.

To eliminate this problem, you can use an anti-seize compound. There are different brands and different formulas, but this helpful compound is usually made of extremely fine particles of powdered aluminum mixed in a lubricant. When a tiny amount is applied to threads a temperature resistant barrier is created that helps keep the two metals from welding themselves together.

Strip Caulk

Often called "dumdum" by mechanics, strip caulk is an extremely versatile and useful caulking compound. It is marketed in strips that can be used to caulk a hole where a hose or cable must pass through sheet metal or to plug a small leak. In an emergency, it can be used to hold parts in position temporarily. For example, it can control an electrical short circuit by holding bare wires apart, or it can hold a loose mirror in place. It's a sort of professional bubble gum, that sticks to almost anything. You'll find it at parts stores for about five dollars a pound.

Buying Car Parts

Types of parts: The three basic options for repair parts are new, remanufactured, and used parts.

New parts are available from car dealers and auto parts stores, remanufactured parts are usually available at auto parts stores only, and used parts are found at wrecking yards.

To make a decision between new or remanufactured parts for your car, consider the difference in price, the identity and reputation of the remanufacturer, and the kind of warranty you'll get. Remanufactured parts will cost at least 25 percent less than new ones, and you may be getting high quality for a lot less money.

In some cases, the remanufacturers are the same companies as the original equipment manufacturers, rebuilding their own components. Most of the time, though, they are smaller, local companies that specialize in a few kinds of car parts.

Auto parts remanufacturing should not be confused with the sometimes shoddy "rebuilding" of the part. This rebuilding process is generally not as reliable as a thorough remanufacturing. A remanufactured alternator, for example, only uses the old case, armature shaft, and winding frames. The old copper windings are removed, and new wire, new bearings, new diodes, and new terminals are installed. The finished product is bench tested before being packed. It is the mechanical and electrical equivalent of a new alternator, and it carries the same warranty.

Parts stores: There are two basic types of parts stores, wholesale and retail.

Retail parts stores are either local or part of a national chain. The national chain varieties look like modern hardware or department stores, and the local stores often resemble an old fashioned hardware stores. A typical retail parts store will stock over 100,000 parts.

Wholesale stores, which are often open to the public, can stock as many as one million parts. At a wholesale store, you usually place an order for a part at a desk. The clerks have access to huge catalogues, which help them find the right for your car. Although mechanics usually pay wholesale prices at these stores, a do-it-yourselfer must usually pay the retail price.

Used parts are generally purchased at a wrecking yard. Most of us want to save money any way we can, and many wrecked cars have good parts at substantial savings. On large parts, such as engines or transmissions, a wrecking yard can save you 50 percent of the cost of a new unit. When buying a used part, carefully check out your guarantee and return privileges in case the part doesn't work or doesn't fit properly.

Deciding what type of part to buy will depend largely on the part itself. For parts that wear out periodically, such as wiper blades, spark plugs, ignition points, and other low cost items, always buy new. Parts such as wheel covers, bumpers, body sections, and trim, are perfectly acceptable used. In addition to the savings, they often fit better than new parts.

Emergencies

Driving a car, sooner or later an emergency will arise. You can't anticipate every possible mishap, but being prepared is your best form of preventive maintenance.

Every car should have a first aid kit and a few supplies. The kit doesn't have to be elaborate, but it should be sealed and include bandages, adhesive tape, and gauze. You should also, carry a pack of at least three safety flares, a flashlight, and an old towel. If you've never lit a safety flare, buy an extra flare and ignite it for practice over a clear concrete area. You won't want to have to learn how to use a safety flare during a real emergency.

If you are planning a trip, some other important items include a gallon of water, a quart of oil, and transmission fluid, if you have an automatic transmission. Tip: Wrap as many of your supplies as possible in an old towel and tie it to keep the tools from rattling around your trunk.

There are a few other items that you might consider keeping in your trunk. Blocks of wood to place under the tire diagonally across from a flat to ensure that the car won't move while jacked up. Many people keep fire extinguishers in their homes to use in an emergency; this safety measure is also important in your car. Jumper cables are easy to use, as described in Chapter 6, and they can save you the typical $50 fee that service stations often charge.

In this book, you will learn how to change engine belts, so carry an extra of the ones that you may need. Even if you don't do it yourself, having the right belt for your cars can sometimes mean the difference between a quick repair and waiting at a service station for three hours, or overnight, while the right part is found.

After you learn how to check and fill your car's fluids, keep the proper engine oil, antifreeze, transmission fluid, power steering fluid, and windshield washer fluid in your trunk to keep you going until you are at a place where a leak can be discovered and fixed.

Supplies for Snow and Ice

In the fall, make sure you have the proper winter supplies in your car. Your equipment should include an inexpensive folding shovel, a snow brush, an ice scraper, and sand. Carry the sand in plastic gallon milk bottles to keep it from spilling. The bottles will make it easy to pour the sand right where you want it.

Never carry salt in your trunk because moisture may cause it to react with the metal or rug in your trunk. Sand is just as effective and works much faster.

Duct Tape

Duct tape is a grey fabric adhesive that can patch up almost anything. It can temporarily hold together a ruptured water hose until a more permanent solution is available. It can also be a great way to hold your trunk closed when it's over-loaded or the latch is broken. It can even be used to make the letters for a Help sign that would be visible at night because of the duct tape's reflecting qualities.

Safety

The repair jobs in this book are not hazardous. Nevertheless, there is always the potential for injury when working with tools. Here are some basic safety tips for working on your car:

1. Never work in a hurry. Plan your work, and anticipate the result of each action. If you're tackling an unfamiliar job, read the instructions and don't hesitate to discuss the procedure with a mechanic.

2. Always use the right tool for any job. Avoid pliers and adjustable wrenches for tightening or loosening bolts. They can slip and cause an injury. Use the correct size tools and take care of them. Never set a tool down on the floor, even for an instant. Slipping on a forgotten tool on the floor, especially while carrying something heavy can be a disaster. Keep your tools clean.

3. Have plenty of light on the project. A light with a clip that fits onto a piece of the car and can be shone in a specific direction is terrific.

4. Never trust a bumper jack!! Never put any part of your body under a car supported only by a bumper jack. Every tool shop or parts store sells inexpensive safety jack stands. Use the bumper jack only to raise the car, then settle it solidly on the jackstands before crawling under it.

5. Always wear safety goggles. Good ones are not very expensive and should be worn even by people who wear eyeglasses. Many of the fluids around an automobile are corrosive to the eyes. In addition, metal and plastic particles, dirt and debris, especially from under a car, can be dangerously abrasive.

6. Use a mask when doing dusty or smoky work. They are inexpensive and disposable

Remember: *Safety comes first!*

Keeping It Going

3

Preventive maintenance is the key to keeping your car healthy. While many repair problems are due to faulty design and assembly, most mechanics agree that the most important cause of today's high repair bills is the failure to conduct regular maintenance checks on your car. Ignoring those squeaking brakes can mean the difference between a $79 set of replacement brake pads and a $475 brake job. A regular $14.95 oil change can prevent a major engine overhaul and add years to your engine's life.

Throughout this book, you'll learn how to repair your car and deal with problems. But this chapter will help you prevent those problems from occurring in the first place. We'll tell you how to check each of the systems and how to make your car last. We have also provided a summary of twenty-five key checks to keep you on the road.

Keep a log of all the maintenance work done on your car. This history can be a money saving diagnostic tool. Most drug and department stores carry inexpensive car cost logs.

In This Chapter...

Preventing Trouble	Breaking In a New Car
Extending Your Car's Life	Weather and Your Car

Our list of easy-to-do maintenance checks and tips will help you keep your car in top shape.

The first time you read it, you may want to have your owner's manual handy so you can find the exact locations of the items mentioned. The owner's manual provides directions to many do-it-yourself checks as well as your car's schedule of preventive maintenance. (Warning: Not following the recommendations in the owner's manual may void your warranty.) If you don't have a copy of the manual, try contacting the manufacturer's Parts and Service Department at the address listed at the back of this book.

We've also included a handy reference table listing when to do what. We've tried to be conservative, so that if you don't do a check when we suggest, you're *not* endangering your car or your life. However, following the schedule can definitely reduce operating costs and keep your car running smoothly.

For more detailed information on these items, see their corresponding inspection and repair sections later in the book.

Oil:

o   Check the oil every 1,000 miles. Motor oil is your car's lifeblood, and this item is the single most important maintenance check you can do.

To check the oil, remove the oil dipstick, wipe it clean, reinsert it, and remove it again. The dipstick will show you how much oil you have. The oil line should be between the "ADD" and "FULL" marks. Add oil if it is needed. You should do this check when the engine is off but warm.

o   Change your oil every 3,000 to 5,000 miles. Regular oil changes are the next most important way to keep your car running. Oil eventually wears out when its additives are depleted, and the chemicals built up can contaminate and deteriorate your engine.

o   Because your oil filter plays a key role in keeping your oil free of large particles, it is important to change the oil filter every time your oil is changed. Buying top graded, SF, oil is another way to pamper your engine, because it provides the best anti-wear properties.

Accessories:

o   Keep the windshield washer reservoir full, and replace your wiper blades when they streak. This check is actually more for safety while driving than for maintenance.

o   After washing your car, check the trunk, windows, sunroof, and floor carpeting for leaks.

Tires:

o   Check your tire pressure monthly, keeping tires inflated to the maximum recommended pressure written on the side of tire. Give them the penny test and look for tread wear bars. Check for cuts and bulges. Having healthy tires can improve tire wear, fuel consumption, and vehicle handling.

o   Test your shocks by bouncing the car up and down. If the car bounces three times, your shocks need to be replaced. Have the front end greased and the alignment and wheel bearing serviced. Front end problems are not only expensive to repair, but they can be safety hazards. Conduct this check when you suspect a problem, or every 12,000 miles.

Fluids:

o Check the transmission fluid every 12,000 to 15,000 miles. With your engine warm and running and the parking brake on, shift to drive, then to park. Remove the dipstick, wipe it dry, reinsert, and pull it out again. Add fluid if needed, but be careful not to overfill.

You should change the transmission fluid every 40,000 miles. This change can greatly reduce the incidence of transmission repairs.

o Check your brake fluid monthly. First, use a rag to clean off the brake master cylinder reservoir lid. Pry off the retainer clip and remove the lid. If you need fluid, be sure to use the type recommended by the manufacturer. If you have to add fluid often, ask a mechanic to check for leaks.

o Check the power steering fluid once a month. Simply remove the reservoir dipstick. If the level is down, add power steering fluid.

o Periodically check under the car for leaking fluids and for loose or broken exhaust clamps and supports. Look for holes in the muffler when the car is running. If you have a leakage problem, park your car over a few sheets of newspaper for a night. When you back the car off the papers, inspect them for leaking fluids. Watery and greenish fluid is probably from your radiator; if it's reddish and greasy, it is probably from your transmission or power steering pump. Brake fluid is light brown, and the darkest fluid is probably oil. Any of these leaks should be checked out. If you notice clear, clean water dripping out from under your car, it is the normal condensation from your air conditioner.

Belts:

o Inspect belts monthly. Replace worn, cracked or frayed belts. Push down on the belts, and have them tightened if they have more than one half inch of slack.

Filters:

o Check the air filter every two months. It is an important check and an easy part to replace.

Fuel System:

o Inspect your engine once a month for accumulated oil or grease, which could indicate a leaky gasket or oil filter.

o Have your carburetor cleaned and overhauled every 48,000 miles.

o Be sure the valve lash is adjusted correctly. It should be checked every 24,000 miles or if you hear an unusual tapping noise. Ignore this adjustment, and an expensive valve job is a certainty.

o Keep a running tab on your fuel economy. A drop in your mileage could signal engine problems or the need for a tune-up. If keeping a running average is impractical for you, check it every 5,000 miles.

Electric System:

o Check the battery monthly. Make sure the cables are securely attached and free of corrosion. Open the caps and check the fluid level. Add water if needed. Caution: Never smoke or light a match near the battery.

o Check your lights monthly, including brake lights, turn signals, and emergency flashers. As you check them, wipe them off with a wet rag. Also, take a moment to check your dashboard warning lights. When you turn the key one notch, do they all work? Your owner's manual will tell you which ones should light up.

Cooling System:

o Check the anti-freeze/coolant level monthly. Most newer cars have plastic tanks next to the radiator with level markings. If the fluid is low, fill the tank up with a 50/50 solution of permanent anti-freeze and water.
   Caution: Do not remove the radiator cap when engine is hot.

o Inspect the radiator and heater hoses every two months. Check the clamps, and look for leaks, cracks, and swelling.

o Flush out your radiator and change your thermostat every two years.

Brakes:

o Check your brakes and parking brake monthly. Push the brake pedal down; it should feel like you are hitting something hard. If it moves more than halfway to the floor without stopping, or if it feels soft, have your brakes checked; there may be air in the brake lines.

o Also check the many metal parts of the brake lines for rust.

o Have your disk brake rotor inspected. This check can prevent having to replace the expensive rotor along with the inexpensive pads. It should be checked every 24,000 miles.

Preventive Maintenance Checklist						
What to Do, Change or Check	When to Do It (mileage)					
	1,000	2,000	5,000	12,000	24,000	48,000
Oil Check	X					
Oil Change			X			
Oil Filter Change			X			
Battery Check	X					
Lighting Check	X					
Coolant Level Check	X					
Coolant Flush and Change					X	
Engine Hose Check		X				
Brake Fluid Check	X					
Brake Check (self)	X					
Brake Check (professional)					X	
Power Steering Fluid Check	X					
General Fluid Leak Check	X					
Belt Check	X					
Air Filter Check		X				
Washer Fluid Check	X					
Tire Pressure Check	X					
Shock Absorber Check				X		
Engine Coolant Check	X					
Carburetor Check (professional)						X
Valve Check					X	
Gas Mileage			X			

Note: We've used mileage to mark when these important checks should be made. If keeping track by calendar is easier for you, then, on the average, 1,000 miles is equivalent to one month.

Breaking In a New Car

Whether you have a new car or a car with a reconditioned engine, the initial break-in is a key factor in ensuring a long and efficient life. In fact, a number of expensive repairs can be attributed to improper break-in. Even though your warranty may cover some of these expenses, problems resulting from improper break-in can often surface after the warranty has expired.

Here are some tips to keep in mind when breaking in your car. Following them for at least the first 500 miles, and preferably the first 2,000 miles, will substantially extend your car's life.

1. During the first 500 miles, long trips are far better than numerous short ones. Vary the speed every few miles so that the engine can break in at different speeds.

2. Try not to accelerate rapidly during the break-in period. Also, do not decelerate rapidly from high speeds.

For example, suddenly letting up on the gas at highway speeds can put an extra strain on your transmission.

3. Check your owner's manual for maximum break-in speeds. If your car has a manual transmission, the break-in speeds will be listed for each gear and are generally lower than the recommended speeds for after break-in.

4. Do not warm-up the engine. Keep your idle time to the absolute minimum. More oil circulates at running speeds than at idle, and you want maximum lubrication during break-in. (Note: In severely cold weather, it *is* advisable to warm up the engine, but only for a minute.)

5. Check your owner's manual for the number of times to depress the accelerator pedal prior to starting. This may vary from the car you are used to, and you could flood the engine or cause the starter to work unnecessarily.

6. Check your coolant level before you leave the show room and after the first 25 miles or so of driving. Often the coolant has not been topped off, and overheating is one of the worst things you can do to a new engine.

7. If you have power steering, avoid holding the wheel at its extreme left or right, or you will strain the power steering pump.

8. Avoid using the air conditioner during the 500 mile break-in period. After break-in, try to turn off the air conditioner a few minutes before you stop the car to allow the engine to run at a cooler temperature.

9. Avoid trailer towing during the break-in period.

10. Remember that your brakes and tires are not as efficient during the first few hundred miles as they will be later, so allow extra room for stopping.

Driving to Extend Your Car's Life

In addition to regular maintenance and initial break-in, the way you drive can affect the life of your car. Practicing the following tips can substantially extend your car's life.

1. Never ride with your foot on the brake, and always remember to release your parking brake. Use the same foot on the accelerator and the brake to avoid being a two-footed driver. Also, avoid sudden stops, as heavy use of the brakes will dramatically shorten their life.

2. Do not crank your starter motor for over 15 seconds at a time. Continual cranking causes the starter motor to overheat and shortens its life.

3. Your owner's manual will have recommendations for severe driving conditions. You may be surprised that "severe" driving is not long distances at high speeds, but stop and go, around town driving. Short trips, combined with rapid acceleration, are hard work for your car.

A car driven primarily on the highway is more likely to be in top condition than one with half the mileage that has been driven only around town. If you regularly drive in stop and go conditions, treat your car to a freeway trip for at least 15 minutes a week.

4. If you regularly carry heavy loads (in your trunk or trailer) and other drivers signal that your high beams are on, you may need heavy duty shock absorbers to keep your car at the proper level.

5. Start your engine before you turn on lights or other electrical items to direct all of your battery's starting power to the starter.

6. Do not use the temporary spare tire longer than is absolutely necessary. These smaller tires put an extra strain on your suspension system and can throw your car out of alignment.

7. Avoid letting the engine idle with the transmission in gear. Put the car in neutral and use the emergency brake, or shift into park.

8. Don't shift your automatic transmission into gear if the engine is running at high speed. A hard clunk when you shift means you're either giving too much gas or your engine is idling too high. A quick tap on the gas pedal can slow down your idle.

9. With manual transmission, always push the clutch pedal fully to the floor when shifting. Also, try to keep your hand off the shift lever while driving. If you stop at a light for more than 30 seconds, put the transmission in neutral, and take your foot off the clutch to avoid overheating. Avoid using the clutch to hold you on a hill. Keeping the pedal slightly depressed increases the wear on your clutch and shortens its life. Even with an automatic transmission, don't hold the car on a hill by slightly accelerating.

Check your owner's manual for the proper speed for shifting manual transmissions. Using the wrong gear increases fuel consumption and strains the engine.

10. Don't adjust your driving habits to compensate for changes in the way your car handles. For example, don't start pumping the brakes harder if they get softer, and don't overcorrect steering if the car pulls in one direction. Have the problems checked out; your car is telling you something.

11. Try to avoid short trips, which are expensive because they usually involve a cold vehicle. For the first mile or two, a cold vehicle gets just 30 to 40 percent of the mileage that it gets when fully warm. After an engine runs for 10 to 15 minutes without interruption, it is usually fully warmed up.

In addition to being inefficient, short trips generate the most wear and tear on your engine.

Weather and Your Car

Summer heat: You can keep your tires cool in the summer by maintaining their recommended air pressure. Heat--not nails, glass, or other sharp objects--is a tire's greatest enemy. Make sure to check tire pressure when the tires are cold, because heat increases tire pressure readings.

Driving in rain: Slow down in the rain to avoid hydroplaning, which occurs when the tires lose contact with the road and ride on top of the water. Be particularly careful during the first rain after a dry spell. Oil and grease that have accumulated on the road will become quite slick after the first drizzle. This first rain is a prime time for auto accidents.

To cold start the engine: In colder weather, your battery weakens, the oil thickens, and gasoline loses volatility. As a result, the starter turns the engine more slowly, and the gas is harder to ignite. This combination can cause difficulty in starting the engine.

Consult your owner's manual to find how many times the accelerator pedal should be depressed before turning on the ignition or if it should be pressed at all. This method varies from car to car, but it should solve the problem.

Snow on the roof: If your car is covered with snow, be sure to clear off the entire car, including the headlights and roof, before driving. As the snow on the roof melts, it can slip down suddenly onto the windshield while you are driving. Not only does this present a safety hazard, but if your wipers are on or you try to use them to clear the snow, they may break.

Getting unstuck in snow: However careful you may be, you will probably get stuck in snow sometime. If you get stuck, try to avoid spinning the wheels. A single rotation of the wheels may be enough to get the car out of the snow under its own power. Put the car in gear and press the accelerator very gently. If that doesn't work, try to "rock" your car out by putting your

foot on and off the gas. But don't let the wheels spin for more than ten or fifteen seconds. When rocking, let your foot off the gas the instant the car stops its forward rock. Turn off all your accessories and roll down the windows so you can listen to the wheels.

If you have front wheel drive, turning the wheels to one side or the other will often provide enough traction to get unstuck.

Supplies for snow and ice: Sometime in the fall, make sure you have the proper winter supplies in your car. Your equipment should include an inexpensive folding shovel, a snow brush, an ice scraper, and sand. Carry the sand in a plastic gallon milk bottle to keep it from spilling. The bottle also makes it easy to pour the sand right where you want it. One bottle should usually be enough.

Never carry salt in your trunk. Moisture can cause the salt to react with the metal or rug in your trunk. Sand is just as effective as salt, and it works much faster.

4

The three key systems in your car, mechanical, fuel, and electric, all meet under the hood. In this chapter, we'll concentrate on the mechanical.

When you first take a peek under the hood, you may question whether you should tackle what's under there. As intimidating as the first look may be, what you're looking at, in concept, has remained essentially unchanged since the first automobiles became popular. The parts have just become much more sophisticated. You probably would not think of working on most of what you see, and you should not try. However, there are repairs that you *can* do, and understanding what's there will go a long way to ensure that you have repairs done fairly and inexpensively.

In this chapter, we'll provide the basics on reasonable repairs. We've tried to be as generic as possible, and every car has the parts we're discussing. While the part may not be identical to what we've shown, it will be there; otherwise your car wouldn't go.

In This Chapter...

What's Under There   The Emission Control System
The Transmission   The Filters
The Cooling System   The Belts
The Oil System

What's Under There?

Obviously, the first thing you find under the hood is the engine. On front wheel drive cars, the engine usually, but not always, is mounted transversely (side to side). On rear wheel drive cars, the engine runs front to back.

The heart of your car is the *internal combustion engine* which mixes gasoline and air and ignites it to turn a shaft which then powers the wheels. This combustion occurs in the four, six, or eight cylinders that most engines have.

Under the hood, you also find most of the key components in the electrical system (see Chapter Six), the cooling system, the transmission and other miscellaneous and sundry parts, such as the belts, the oil dipstick, and the filters.

In this section, we'll tell you about everything you need to know and how to examine and repair the simpler components.

Remember, repairs that are simple for you are even simpler for a mechanic, so they can represent some of your biggest money savers.

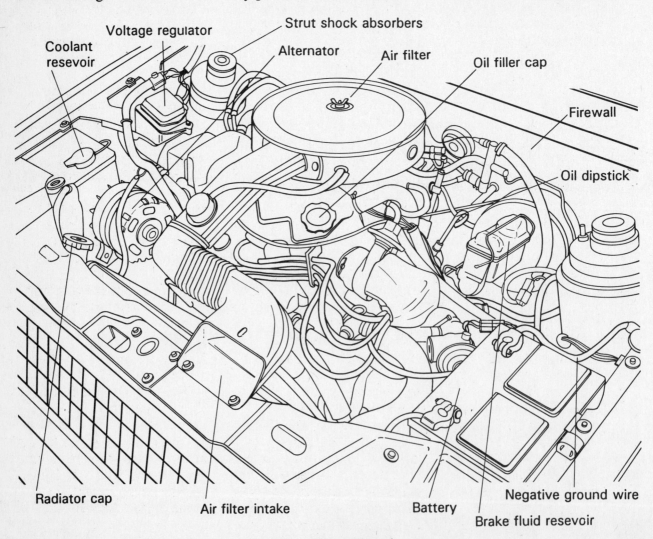

Engine Compartment

The Transmission

The transmission is made up of a series of gears which control the power of the engine to your wheels. It allows the engine to function efficiently at high speeds and provides extra power for starting and quick acceleration.

Similar in concept to the gears on a ten speed bicycle, the lower gears allow the engine to turn faster for the extra power needed to accelerate from a stop or to climb a steep hill and the higher gears (used at high speeds) let the engine run more slowly for longer life and better fuel economy.

On rear wheel drive cars, the transmission is between the engine and the drive shaft. The drive shaft goes to the differential (which allows the outside wheels to rotate faster than the inside wheels in a turn) and then to the wheels.

On front-wheel drive cars, a single unit called a transaxle incorporates both the transmission and the differential. Without a differential, the car would skid in every turn and tire wear would be extremely rapid.

Most cars sold in America have automatic transmissions, but manual transmissions are still found on economy and sports cars. With proper care, either type of transmission can last as long as you own your car and, at the very least, you can keep expenses associated with this complicated device to a minimum.

Automatic transmission:
As the name implies, an automatic transmission shifts the gears for you according to the speed of the engine and the power required. It is an amazing device and, as you can imagine, extremely complicated. Replacing an automatic transmission is one of the most expensive car repair jobs, so there's a big incentive to keep it in top shape. You should have the automatic transmission serviced every 25,000 miles.

Here are two tips for making your transmission last:

1. Use the first gear, (L1 or low), for hard pulling, snow and mud or climbing steep grades.

2. Do not shift into neutral and coast. Driving in neutral gives you no control over the car, (it's illegal in some states), and is unsafe. Coasting could also increase the load on the brakes and damage the transmission.

Manual transmission:
This type of transmission is much simpler because the unit does not have to calculate the correct time to shift--you do. Manual transmissions are exceptionally durable and repairs are usually focused on the clutch which temporarily disengages the transmission from the engine while you change gears. Clutches go through a tremendous amount of stress, and they often need to be replaced during the life of the car. However, they are not nearly as expensive to replace as an entire transmission. If a clutch goes too long without adjustment, it will begin to slip, and the engine will race as if it were in neutral.

How to check out your manual transmission: Always be sure the clutch pedal is loose enough to push down a half inch to an inch, depending on the car, before the clutch disengages. It should require more pressure yet to push it to the floor. Have your clutch adjusted if the amount of play exceeds one inch.

In order to make your manual transmission last as long as possible:

1. Do not "rev" the engine for more than 10 seconds while the brakes are on or the clutch is engaged.

2. Shift from lower to higher gears as soon as you can but don't exceed the speed limit recommended for each gear in the owner's manual.

Automatic Transmission Fluid Check

Transmission fluid does not wear out or become contaminated with acids, as engine oil does. If your transmission filter is doing its job, if your bands are properly adjusted, and if your fluid is kept at its proper level, your transmission may theoretically last forever.

Checking your fluid level is easy and can prevent an expensive repair job.

Automatic transmission fluid is available at most parts stores. Check the owner's manual or the transmission dipstick for the correct type for your car.

Repair rating: Basic.

What you need: All you'll need is a cloth or paper towel.

What to do:
1. The engine should be warmed up and running with the gear selector in "Park" in order to get an accurate reading.

2. Find the transmission fluid dipstick. Usually it is at the rear of the engine and looks like a smaller version of the oil dipstick.

3. Remove the dipstick and, with a clean cloth or paper towel, wipe it dry. Reinsert it, pull it out and note the level and color of the fluid.

4. If the fluid is below the "add" line, pour in one pint at a time. Be sure not to overfill the reservoir.

5. While checking the fluid, note its color. It should be a bright, cherry red. If it is a darker, reddish brown, the fluid needs changing. If it is very dark, nearly black, and has a burnt smell (like varnish), your transmission may be damaged. You should take it to a specialist.

Manual Transmission Fluid

Fluid levels in both the transmission and differential should be checked with each oil change, or when you notice erratic or rough gear shifting. Both shift problems are signs that the level is low. On most cars, the manual transmission lubricant does not require changing but it should be replenished if it gets low.

Changing Automatic Transmission Fluid

Overheating the transmission, perhaps by towing a heavy load up a steep hill, scorches the automatic transmission fluid (ATF). If this fluid is any color other than a bright, healthy red, or if it smells burned, the fluid should be changed, and the filter must be changed at the same time!

In an automatic transmission, the filter protects the valve bodies, clutches, and internal passageways by cap-turing dirt, dust, grit, or metal contaminants. There are dozens of models of auto-matic transmission filters, vir-tually all of which are inter-nal. You should change the automatic transmission filter every 24,000 miles.

Tip: Beware of national chains who offer free trans-mission fluid check and then recommend a major repair. If you check your fluid regu-larly and don't notice any performance problems, your transmission is fine.

Note: Changing your Automatic Transmission Fluid using this method does *not* change the fluid in the torque converter, which is the mechanism located inside the transmission that converts the engine's rotational energy into energy suitable for the drive line. Only a profes-sional shop should attempt this.

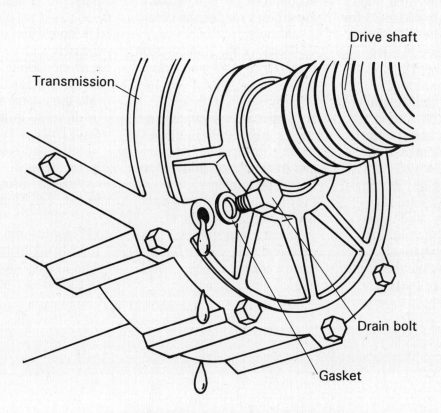

Changing the Transmission Fluid
View From Under The Car

Repair rating: Adventuresome.

What you need: You'll need a "kit" containing the exact replacement filter plus the gasket for the transmission pan. All filter kits come with excellent instructions and diagrams. More instructions for your specific vehicle may be found in the shop manual, and major libraries have good collections of shop manuals. Also, you'll need several quarts of the correct type of new transmission fluid; consult your Owner's Manual for type and quantity. The job will require a good lifting jack (your bumper jack will do) plus two sturdy jack stands rated to the weight of the vehicle. You'll need a ratchet wrench and a selection of sockets, a wrench for the drain plug, a few other small tools depending on your make and model car, some rags, gasket adhesive, and a container to catch the old fluid. The instructions included in the kit will indicate the exact type and sizes of tools you will need.

What to do:
1. Read the instructions that come with the kit. Jack the car up and position the safety jacks stands.

2. Get underneath, find the transmission pan, and wipe the area clean.

3. Remove the drain plug and capture as much fluid as will flow out. The drain plug for an automatic transmission will be on the bottom of the transmission pan, at the lowest point of the pan, usually toward the rear of the car.

4. Remove the transmission pan. More ATF will drain out.

5. Use a gasket scraper or strong putty knife to clean the mating surfaces of the pan and transmission body. Caution: The transmission body may be aluminum; do not use a sharp steel scraper. Acetone (wear gloves!) is an excellent solvent for stubborn gasket adhesive.

6. Clean out any debris in the bottom of the pan. Wipe all surfaces clean and dry.

7. Remove the old filter following instructions.

8. Install the new filter, following the instructions with the filter.

9. Apply the gasket adhesive to adhere the new gasket to the pan and reinstall the pan and bolts, tightening them evenly. Reinstall the drain plug and gasket.

10. Lower the car and put in the new fluid. The correct amount should be in your owner's manual. Start and idle the engine for 15 minutes or drive 10 miles. Check the fluid level with the engine running and transmission selector in park. Add fluid as required to bring the level up to the "full" mark.

11. Inspect under the car for fluid leaks from the pan gasket. If you spot any, gently re-tighten the pan bolts.

The Cooling System

Automobile engines generate enough heat to warm a six-room house in freezing temperatures. In cars with smaller radiators, air conditioning, or crowded engine compartments, the temperatures under the hood may rise to over 280 degrees.

In order to keep the engine cool, the engine block is surrounded by a blanket of flowing coolant (usually a 50/50 mixture of water and antifreeze) which draws heat away from the engine and into the radiator. Air blows across the radiator and cools the hot water before it returns to the engine. The diagram displays the various parts of this important system.

If the cooling system fails, the engine will become so hot that the parts will expand to the point where they would simply cease to move. Ironically, mechanics call this superheated condition "freezing-up."

A well operating cooling system is one of the most crucial elements in prolonging the life of the engine, yet it is one of the simplest systems on the car. It consists of a radiator, which spreads the water out so it can be cooled by the air, rubber hoses, which carry the water to and from the engine, the heater, which draws in the hot engine water to heat the inside of the car, the thermostat, which controls the flow of water through the engine in order to maintain the optimum operating temperature, the water pump, which keeps the water moving through the system, either a mechanical or electric fan, and a radiator pressure cap which maintains the cooling system pressure.

What can go wrong: Problems in the cooling system are usually due to leakage. Cracked hoses, holes in the radiator or a leaky gasket in the engine can cause a gradual loss of coolant until there is not enough to effectively cool the engine. Another typical problem involves a loose or broken water pump belt which stops the coolant from circulating through the engine. A clogged radiator may also cause overheating. You can confirm that your radiator is clogged by simply removing the lower hose from it and trying to run water through it.

When a water pump stops working, you will sometimes hear the grinding of the bearings. This is often caused by a belt that's too tight or coolant water leaking into the pump's mechanical parts.

If a radiator cap is not maintaining pressure in the cooling system, the engine may not run at its optimum efficiency--the boiling point decreases and coolant begins to boil off. This could result in overheating. The most common reasons for pressure cap failure are the rubber seal's and pressure release valve's deteriorating over time. This problem requires replacement of the cap. Replacing a worn pressure cap is easy and requires only a few minutes.

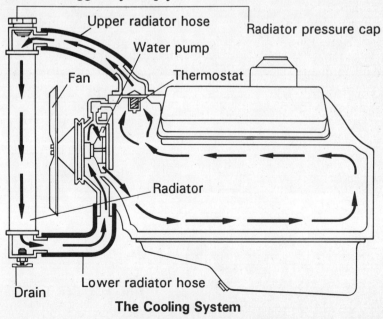

The Cooling System

Cooling System Checks and Warning Signs

Because the cooling system is so important to your engine, it is important to make sure that the system is operating at its fullest level at all times.

o Keep your radiator clean by spraying it with a hose from the engine side. The bugs and other debris that get caught in it can reduce air flow and cooling efficiency. Look for leaks and cracks.
o Keep the proper tension on the water pump belt to prevent it from failing. Press down on the middle of the belt. It shouldn't give more than about half an inch. Twist the water pump belts around to inspect them underneath.
o Keep the right amount of coolant in the system.
o Keep an eye open for these warning signs of cooling system trouble:

1. Screeching belts when you "rev" the engine;

2. Hose connections on the radiator that look wet or greenish fluid under your car;

3. The engine continues to run for a few seconds after the ignition has been turned off;

4. The engine knocks or "pings" when accelerating.

Three and four may also signify an improper grade of fuel or need for an engine tune-up.

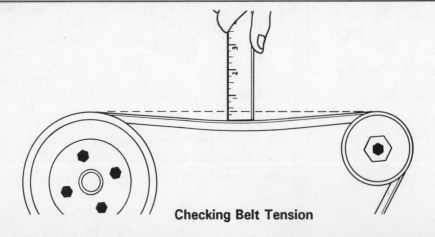

Checking Belt Tension

Coolant

Once a month or every 1,000 miles, whichever comes first, check the level of the coolant in the radiator. Whenever you tow a trailer or boat, check the level daily. Coolant level should be checked on a cold engine.

Use a 50/50 mix of anti-freeze and water in your coolant system. That mix is appropriate for most of the United States; it freezes at 60 degrees below zero fahrenheit, and with a pressure cap, its boiling point is well above 250 degrees fahrenheit. It cools well in hot weather and protects well in winter. In certain frigid climates, you may need more anti-freeze.

Caution: Checking the coolant in a hot engine can be extremely dangerous. Scalding hot water and steam can come out of the radiator. If there is a chance that the engine is hot, cover the radiator cap with a heavy cloth. Turn it counter clockwise to the first stop and let the pressure release. The pressure is gone when the hissing stops. Push down on the cap and turn it one quarter turn counterclockwise to release it, and then an additional quarter turn without downward pressure to remove it.

It is also important to check the color of the fluid in the cooling system. If it's clear, it is OK. If it is cloudy or rusty, the system needs to be flushed and refilled.

Many late-model cars have a coolant recovery system. This plastic bottle, attached to the radiator, saves coolant that would normally overflow. It will automatically be drawn back into the radiator when the coolant cools down. On the coolant recovery tank, you should find markings that say "Full Hot" and "Full Cold." If coolant level with both a hot and cold engine is as indicated, everything is OK. If not, add coolant and check for leaks.

It is important to drain and flush the entire system every 24,000 miles to fight rust and corrosion. Most service stations have the equipment to give your cooling system a "reverse flush," the most effective way to clean out the system.

Every parts store sells "Flush and Fill" kits, which come with illustrated instructions. Specific directions vary from one make and model to another, and different brands of kits have slightly different parts and instructions.

Caution: Do not allow the old coolant mixture to drain onto the ground or into a sewer. It's toxic, especially to pets and small children, who like its taste because it's sweet. It's also environmentally damaging to the water supply.

If your car has been losing water or frequently overheating, you may have been topping off the fluid level with water. As a result the coolant/water mix may no longer be 50/50. Flushing and refilling the system will ensure you have properly balanced coolant fluid.

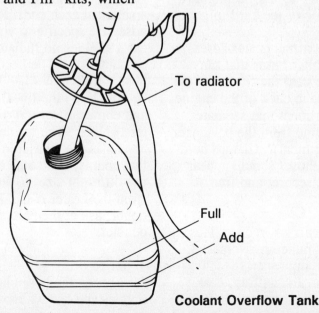

To radiator

Full

Add

Coolant Overflow Tank

Checking the Hoses

Hoses carry coolant mixture from the water pump to radiator, from the radiator back to the engine block, from the water pump to the heater core and back to the engine.

The top radiator hose (which generally needs more frequent replacement) is the easiest to check. It generally returns hot coolant from the engine, so it is subject to the highest temperatures. The radiator's bottom hose, which generally handles cooler water, is the supply hose. It supplies radiator-cooled coolant to the engine.

With the engine cold, physically check each one by squeezing it along its entire length. If a hose is soft and mushy or hard and brittle, then have it replaced.

Hoses should be pliable and free of cracks or swellings. You may need a flashlight to see some of the hard-to-get-at hoses.

Look at the heater hoses, the smaller hoses that run back toward the fire wall (the wall at the back of the engine compartment that separates the engine from the passenger compartment). Clamps holding the hoses should appear strong, secure, and free of rust.

What can go wrong: Hoses can get punctured, cracked, or have improperly installed clamps. In addition, heat, oil, and age can combine in different ways to cause a hose to leak. Note: A feeling of sponginess or an obvious bulge, signals that the hose should be replaced as a preventive measure.

Repair rating: Beyond Basic.

What you need: You'll need the replacement hose or hoses, a sharp knife, a set of cutting "nippers," and replacement hose clamps if the originals are severely rusted. To remove the hose you will need one or more of the following depending on the kind of clamps it has: a nut driver, a screwdriver, a small wrench or socket, or pliers.

Purchase the new hose or hoses and make sure they are the exact fit in terms of diameter, length, and shape. Note: Some are different diameters at each end! Radiator hoses are specific to your car's engine and radiator combination. The heater hose, on the other hand, may be bought by the lineal foot, and comes in several diameters. Note: The inside diameter is the measurement that counts, and some cars use different sizes to and from the heater core. If in doubt, ask at the parts counter.

What to do:
1. Loosen the hose clamps. Screw-type clamps may be removed with a nut driver, with a screwdriver, or a small wrench or socket. Corbin Clamps must be removed only with special Corbin Clamp pliers which you can buy or rent. Attempting to remove these clamps with regular pliers can result not only in damage to your car, but in personal injury as well. The only advantage of Corbin Clamps is that they cost a few cents less. If you discard them and replace them with screw clamps, you'll make your job easier next time.

2. Be prepared to lose some coolant (especially all of it if you're working on the lower hose). Position a container to capture the coolant, which is toxic, and set aside.

3. Remove the old hose. If it is stuck on the soft brass of the radiator or heater core, or on the aluminum of a thermostat housing, be careful pulling it off because it is easy to do expensive damage. A mechanic's trick is to cut off the old hose near the soft fitting, then slit the stub of the hose lengthwise and peel it off.

4. Clean up the fittings from which the hose was removed. Acetone is a suitable solvent for old adhesive, and medium-grit sandpaper or emery cloth will help shine things up for a solid connection.

5. Slip the clamps in position on the new hose, and install the new hose. Tip: A few drops of coolant mixture rubbed inside each end of the hose is an excellent lubricant, and will make the hose slide into place much more easily.

6. Position the clamps close enough to the end of the hose so that they will be snug around the fitting when tightened. If they're too far onto the hose, you will simply tighten onto the hose, and a leak will result. Tighten the clamps carefully and do not overtighten! A screw clamp gives you tremendous mechanical advantage, and you don't want to tear or chew the new hose.

7. If the coolant you removed is relatively clean and clear, you can put it back in the radiator. Start the engine, let it idle for 5 to 10 minutes, and top off as necessary. Be sure the overflow tank is at the "full cold" mark. Replace the radiator cap.

8. Drive for at least 15 minutes. Raise the hood and inspect carefully for leaks. Any leak, no matter how tiny, must be stopped. Otherwise, you risk serious damage to the engine from overheating.

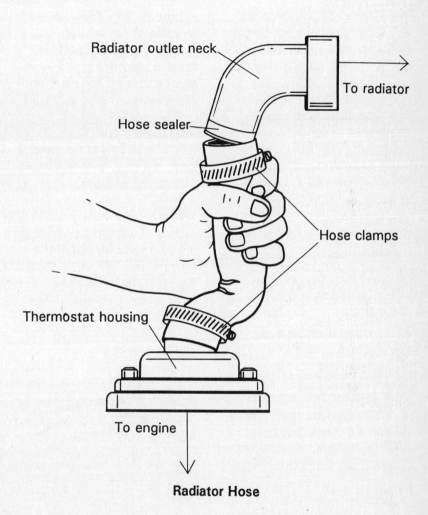

Radiator outlet neck

To radiator

Hose sealer

Hose clamps

Thermostat housing

To engine

Radiator Hose

The Thermostat

The thermostat controls the temperature of the coolant mixture. It's like a valve that opens and closes when the coolant is too hot or too cold. It opens to allow hot coolant into the radiator for cooling and closes to let the water around the engine warm up.

An engine running above or below its normal operating temperature puts an added strain on the parts. If the temperature gauge on your dashboard registers above or below average, it could be the thermostat. Another clue is that your heater doesn't seem to be giving you enough heat.

Thermostat replacement is a quick and easy repair job, and an inexpensive item to replace.

What can go wrong: The thermostat "seat", a seal that's part of the assembly, can become warped or worn. The thermal wax "pellet" that expands at higher temperature to open the thermostat can fail or the spring that holds the thermostat closed can break.

Repair rating: Basic.

What you need: You'll need the correct new thermostat for your engine, a new thermostat gasket and some gasket sealer, the proper wrenches or sockets, and perhaps one or more new hoses.

Buy the exact replacement thermostat for you engine. Double check the part listing rather than automatically replacing it with the same thermostat you removed--someone before you may have installed the wrong one. In addition to the right size and type, make sure the temperature rating is correct.

What to do:
1. To avoid the risk of scalding burns, work only on a cool engine. Overnight cooling is the best.

2. Drain the cooling system. Open the drain valve in the radiator, catch the coolant mixture in a flat pan for re-use.

3. Locate the thermostat housing. Location and appearance vary from one make and model to another, but normally the housing will be toward the top front portion of an engine. It will normally have one large hose (1 1/2 to 2 1/2-inch diameter) connected to it, and possibly another hose about an inch in diameter.

4. Loosen clamps and remove hoses from housing as necessary.

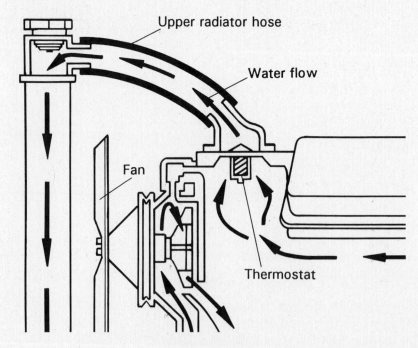

The Thermostat

5. Loosen the mounting nuts and bolts and remove the thermostat housing.

6. Clean off the old gasket material. Tip: Use acetone or gasket removing solvent which parts stores have in small containers. When removing gasket residue be careful not to gouge alumimun parts with sharp tools.

7. Apply gasket sealer according to package directions, and place the new gasket and thermostat in position. Tip: Make sure to install the new thermostat right side up! The package instructions should reassure you. Don't depend on the old one because it may have been upside down!

8. Replace and tighten the thermostat housing and hoses.

9. Top off the radiator with the old coolant mixture, if it's still good. Be sure the Coolant Recovery tank is at the "Full, Cold" mark; replace the radiator cap. Start the engine, allow it to idle 5 to 10 minutes, continuing to top off the coolant as required.

10. Drive for at least 15 minutes, raise the hood and carefully look for leaks. Caution: All coolant leaks, no matter how tiny, must be corrected, or you risk serious damage to you engine as a result of overheating.

Check Your Thermostat

A cold-running engine will dramatically reduce fuel efficiency. Your engine temperature is controlled by a thermostat valve. Most engines are designed to operate efficiently at 180 degrees. An engine running at 125 degrees can waste one out of every ten gallons of gas. If your temperature gauge runs cool or you feel your car should be getting better fuel economy, have your thermostat checked. Thermostats are inexpensive and relatively easy to replace. Running the engine at its proper temperature will increase its life.

The Radiator Cap

A radiator pressure cap keeps the cooling system sealed, and allows pressure to build to the point specified on the cap's label, usually 15 to 17 pounds per square inch. Coolant under pressure can withstand higher temperatures before boiling. As the coolant expands and contracts with changes in temperature, the cap allows coolant to flow between the cooling system and the coolant recovery tank as needed.

What can go wrong: The cap's seal can develop a leak, or the pressure regulating spring can become jammed or broken.

Repair rating: Basic.

What you need: All you need to do this job is the cor-rect replacement radiator cap, a cool engine, and a shop rag. You may also want to have some extra antifreeze handy.

What to do: Always allow the engine to cool down before replacing a radiator cap! Overnight cooling is safest. Attempting this simple repair on a hot or overheated engine can result in serious injury. The coolant mixture can easily be 60 or 70 degrees above the temperature of boiling water, and can inflict dangerous burns.

Buy the exact replacement cap your engine requires. A number of caps may fit physically, but will not work right. Do not simply replace the cap with a new one of the same number (As marked on the cap.) Someone before you may have installed the wrong cap, and you would perpetu-ate the mistake! Your owner's manual may tell you; your dealer or parts store surely will, if you give the the year, make, model, and engine ID for your car.

With the replacement cap at hand and engine cool, place the shop rag over the old cap. Press straight downward on the cap and twist about a quarter-turn counter-clockwise. Release the downward pressure, and rotate counter-clockwise an additional quarter turn. This should allow removal of the old cap. Top off the radiator, if necessary, with a 50/50 mixture of water and anti-freeze. Put the new cap in position, rotate about a quarter-turn clockwise, then apply downward pressure and rotate about another quarter-turn clockwise to "seat" the new cap.

The Fan

The fan helps move air across the radiator to cool the engine. To check the fan, grasp each blade between thumb and fingers, and check for any sign of looseness. The blades are riveted to the hub, and if there is any sign of wear, the entire fan must be replaced.

Caution: Before touching the fan, be sure the ignition switch is off.

If your vehicle has a fan clutch assembly, which should be visible under your hood, there's a separate test. With the ignition off, attempt to rotate the blade. If you push on it and rotation stops within a sixteenth of a turn or so, the clutch is OK. If the fan continues rotating for a quarter turn or more, the clutch is bad. A defective clutch means your engine could overheat.

What can go wrong: Blades may get bent and rivets can work free, resulting in blade looseness. Either condition may produce vibration, which will prematurely wear the water pump and is therefore undesirable. A clutch assembly, found on some fans, may leak or the clutch thermostat may fail.

Repair rating: Adventuresome.

What you need:
You'll need your wrench and socket set and a pry bar to re-tension the belt. The radiator, which is near the fan, has nasty, sharp edges, so wear a pair of heavy canvas gloves. There is a special "fan wrench" with about a 15 inch reach and with a ratcheting socket at its end, made especially for this job. You may be able to rent one, or you may choose to buy one.

What to do:
1. Before working on the fan, disconnect the battery cable at the negative end and tie the terminal in a shop rag. This guarantees that the engine cannot possibly turn over while your hands are involved. There is no need to drain engine coolant.

2. Determine which parts need replacing, and buy them. You may wish to replace the drive belts at this time, as well.

3. Loosen mounting and adjusting bolts as necessary to loosen the drive belt for the fan. Remove the belt.

4. Remove the fan. Even if it's the clutch that's bad, it's easiest to replace it while the fan is off the vehicle. Usually four bolts mount the fan to the front of the water pump; often there's a "spacer" to position the fan closer to the radiator.

5. Remove the old clutch from the fan body, and replace with the new one, if applicable. Usually four bolts mount the clutch to the fan.

6. Replace the fan, being sure to position the spacer properly if there is one. Tighten the mounting bolts. Install the belt, pull it tight with the pry bar, and tighten the adjusting bolt. (See instructions for tightening a belt at the end of this chapter.)

7. When you have completed all the processes that require you to use your hands near the fan, reconnect the battery.

The Electric Fan

The electric fan, like the mechanical fan, draws outside air through the radiator to cool the engine. Electric fans are mostly, but not exclusively, used on cars with small, transverse-mounted (sideways) engines. Unlike a mechanical fan, an electric fan can run at full speed when it's needed most, in slow stop-and-go traffic. The mechanical fan is rotated by a drive belt, and the electrical fan is driven by a motor. When not needed, as at freeway speed, it can turn off and remove its load from the engine; this, in turn, improves mileage. You'll often hear an electric fan running after you shut off your engine and begin to walk away from your car.

What can go wrong: There are two things that can go wrong with your electric fan-- either it won't stop, or it won't run. If the fan motor never stops, there's a short

circuit, probably in the fan thermostat. Check voltage output of the thermostat with the engine thoroughly cold; it should be zero.

Repair rating: Beyond Basic.

What you need: Your wrenches, a pair of "alligator" cables, a pair of common pliers, and a rag.
   Caution: When working on an electric cooling system fan, always disconnect the negative battery terminal and securely wrap it in a shop rag! The fan can start to run at high speed at any moment, even with the ignition turned off.

What to do:
1. If the fan is not working, first check the fuse.

2. If the fuse is OK, disconnect both wires from the fan. Using two alligator cables, connect one wire to the battery's positive (+) terminal

and the other to a reliable "ground" such as the battery's negative (-) terminal or a metal part.

3. If the fan motor doesn't run, then it's bad and must be replaced. Replacing the fan motor varies from car to car, but is a task that can be done at home. If the fan motor is bad, it's usually possible to replace the motor only, by simply attaching the old fan blade's assembly to the new motor.

4. If the fan motor runs when jumped, but not when the engine is hot, you may have a bad fan thermostat. To replace the bad thermostat see the directions earlier in this chapter.

Customer alerts: It is possible to have two defective parts at the same time, for example, a shorted fan motor will almost always blow a fuse.

Oil is the life blood of your engine. Because of all the moving parts, your engine gets very hot. Oil lubricates the moving parts to minimize friction and wear and helps keep the engine cool. As it circulates through the engine block it picks up dirt and small bits of metal that collect inside of the engine. With each pass, the oil goes through a filter which cleans out this debris.

Modern motor oils contain detergent and dispersant additives. The detergents, as you would expect, clean out dirt and grime from the engine, while the dispersants hold them in suspension where they can do little harm. This is what causes the golden brown color of oil to turn dark. Dark oil means that the oil is doing its job, not that it's ready to be changed.

Types of Oil: Your owner's manual will tell you what kind of oil to use in your car. It will be described in terms of a viscosity index. This is a measure of how thick or thin the oil will get at different temperatures.

Higher viscosity (higher numbers) oils are best for warm weather driving because they are thicker and offer better protection against high temperatures. In the winter, lower viscosity (lower numbers) oils are best because they are thinner, and

the thinner oil flows more easily and lubricates the engine better in cold weather.

10W40 is the most common type of oil. The 10W means "10 winter." This oil will be thin enough for your car to turn over easily in cold weather. The "40" is a warm weather measure. The number 40 means that it will be four times as thick in the summer.

The API (American Petroleum Institute) grading system will help you judge the quality of the oil. The grades range from SA (the lowest) to SF (the highest) and include SB, SC, SD and SE. These grades are stamped on each can of oil. SF oils have better anti-wear properties than other grades.

There are synthetic oils on the market today, but they cost two to three times as much as mineral oil. It doesn't make sense to buy them when high quality mineral oils will do an excellent job of protecting your engine. Furthermore, these oils are rated to last 2 to 3 times as long as mineral oils. That may be true, but it misses the point of changing oils to keep your engine clean. If you change your oil every 3,000 to 5,000 miles what good is an expensive oil rated at 10,000 miles?

An engine can leak or burn oil for a number of reasons, some minor, some serious.

Given enough miles and enough time, virtually any engine will begin to burn oil as a result of worn valve guides or worn piston rings, which allow too much space for engine oil to get into the combustion chamber. When the problem becomes serious, either the cylinder head(s) or the complete engine must be rebuilt. However, a defective, incorrect, or improperly installed PCV valve can also cause an otherwise good engine to burn as much as a quart of oil every 100 miles.

An oil leak can result from a loose drain plug, a worn or loose oil pan gasket, a defective fuel pump or other accessory gasket, or worn front or rear main crankshaft seals. All but the worn crankshaft seals are relatively minor and inexpensive to correct. Pinpointing the source of an oil leak can be frustrating.

Checking and Adding Oil: The phrase "fill it up and check the oil" has faded into gas station history. Today, checking the oil is most often the responsibility of the driver. To keep the inner working of your engine clean, you should change your oil at least every 5,000 miles.

To check your oil, first turn off the engine. Find the dipstick. (Look for a loop made of flat wire located on the side of the engine.) If the engine has been running, the dipstick and surrounding engine parts will be hot. You may need a rag to protect your hands. Grab the loop, pull out the dipstick, clean it off with a rag, and reinsert it into the engine. Pull it out again and observe the oil level. You will note the words "full" and "add" marked at the end of the stick. If the level is between "add" and "full" you are OK. If it is below the add mark, you should add enough oil until it reaches the "full" line.

To add oil, remove the cap at the top of the engine block and add the oil that your owners manual recommends. You may have to add more than one quart, but be careful not to put in too much. Overfilling can cause the oil to foam, depriving important parts of the engine of proper lubrication.

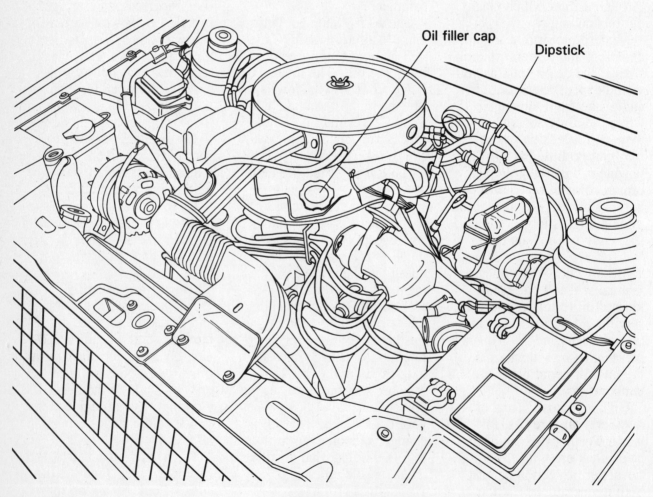

Oil filler cap

Dipstick

Checking Your Oil

Changing the Oil and Filter

Many owner's manuals now contain instructions for changing the oil and filter. If you change the oil in your car's engine, you'll save a few dollars, and you'll learn to know your car a little better.

Repair rating: Beyond Basic

What you need: You'll need only a few tools: a wrench of the proper size for the drain plug, a filter wrench of the right size and style to remove your oil filter, a drain pan to catch the oil, an old plastic jug, and a large funnel.

What to do:
1. Park the car on a level spot, position the drain pan, and remove the plug which is at the lowest point under your engine.

2. After the oil stops dripping, reposition the drain pan and remove the old filter. Be careful, the filter can hold up to a quart of dirty oil.

3. To dispose of the used oil, use the funnel to pour it into the used plastic jug. Carry the old filter in an empty coffee can. Most shops that change oil will accept used oil, and they re-refine it for reuse. Many shops do their space heating with furnaces that burn used oil. You'll find one within two or three

phone calls, and that will solve your disposal problem.

4. Install the new filter, following directions on its label. Replace the drain plug and put in most of the new oil.

5. Run the engine for sixty seconds to pump air out and oil into the new filter, then check the dipstick and fill to the proper level. You're all done.

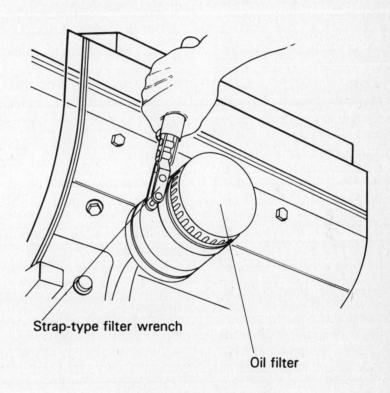

Strap-type filter wrench

Oil filter

Replacing the Oil Filter

On any vehicle, the emission control system attempts what its name describes; it controls exhaust and other vehicle emissions.

The objectionable ingredients in exhaust emissions are unburned hydrocarbons, carbon monoxide, carbon dioxide, and oxides of nitrogen. In addition, there have been problems with sulphur dioxide, phosphorus, lead, and other heavy metals.

Control of these pollutants has been approached by reducing their presence in gasoline. Federal regulations have mandated increasing the use of lead-free fuel, and have encouraged reductions in phosphorus and sulphur content.

Federal regulations mandate more stringent emission limits, to which manufacturers have responded reluctantly but successfully. Many states (with California in the lead) and metropolitan areas have adopted their own standards and require annual emissions inspection, usually at the time of license renewal.

Emission control systems vary greatly from one auto manufacturer to another, from one year to another, and from one vehicle to another, though the objectives are the same and many of the techniques are similar. For example, gasoline is a hydrocarbon, and fuel vapor recovery systems capture gasoline fumes that would otherwise escape into the atmosphere. Other aspects of the emission control are Positive Crankcase Ventilation (PCV) systems, Air Injection Reactor (AIR) systems, and Exhaust Gas Recirculation (EGR) systems.

Computer control of ignition added a new level of precision and complexity to the emission control process, so that the automobile continuously monitors its own exhaust and adjusts the quantity of fuel fed to the cylinders.

Contrary to negative propaganda, emission control does not cause lower fuel economy; the net effect is mileage that is the same or better than it would have been without the system.

Evaluating the effectiveness of emission control systems requires complex and expensive equipment which is used only by professionals, often state-certified emission technicians.

Emission control systems carry a mandatory warranty for at least 50,000 miles, and the warranty extends beyond the original owner. If you buy a low-mileage used car, it pays to keep a reliable history of odometer readings and a complete service history. As your vehicle approaches 50,000 miles, it's wise to have the emissions tested. If defects are discovered, they will be corrected by the dealer at no charge.

More than 90 percent of cars on the road are equipped with catalytic converters. The converter, along with other automotive emissions controls, has reduced hydrocarbons and carbon monoxide emissions by 96 percent from the uncontrolled vehicles of the early 1960's.

PCV: When your car is running, some of the fuel and exhaust fumes get past the piston rings and into the crankcase. Originally, these fumes were put into the atmosphere through a tube so as not to contaminate the oil in the crankcase. To cut down pollution, the Positive Crankcase Ventilation system (PCV) was developed in the sixties. The PCV reroutes the fumes back to the intake manifold to reburn them in the cylinders along with the rest of the air/fuel mixture.

The PCV valve works by allowing engine vacuum to draw a precisely metered amount of fresh air through a breather filter, into the crankcase, and then into the intake manifold, where it combines with the fuel/air mixture. This enables air in the crankcase which was badly contaminated with oil fumes, smoke, and tiny particles of engine oil and formerly vented to the atmosphere to be burned along with the fuel.

PCV

You should check the PCV valve at every tune up, and most manufacturers recommend that you replace the PCV valve after 12,000 miles.

What can go wrong: If the PCV valve is not operating properly, the air/fuel mixture will be out of balance, and your car will not run as efficiently. After 10,000 to 15,000 miles, the PCV valve becomes corroded, worn and contaminated by carbon deposits. It can also become clogged with sludge from contaminants in the fumes, in which case it should be replaced.

Some of the worst symptoms an auto engine can manifest can be caused by a loose, worn, or punctured PCV hose. The indications include: engine misfire on one or more cylinders, producing engine vibration; drastic loss of power and acceleration; atrocious gas mileage; and extreme difficulty starting, especially when cold.

Repair rating: Basic

What you need: Essentially, all you need to replace your PCV valve. There's a huge variety of PCV Valve types and methods of attachment. Some are threaded into a throttle body and must be removed with a wrench. Some thread directly into a manifold, and also require a wrench. Others simply "press fit" into a neoprene "doughnut" in a valve cover, and can be serviced with nothing but hands and a shop rag!

What to do:
1. Find the hose that goes from the bottom of the carburetor to the top of the valve cover or oil filter hole. Some PCV valves screw into the base of the carburetor, some push into a rubber grommet in the cylinder head valve cover at the end of the hose that leads to the carburetor, and others screw or push into the oil filler cap or tube.

2. Keep your engine idling and pinch the hose hard enough to stop the air flowing through it. Be very careful not to puncture the hose. If the PCV is OK, the idle speed should drop obviously, and you'll be able to hear the change.

3. Another way to check the PCV valve is to remove it from the valve cover, with the hose still attached, and place your finger over the opening. If it's working as it should, you will feel a strong suction.

4. If the valve is not working, it must be replaced.

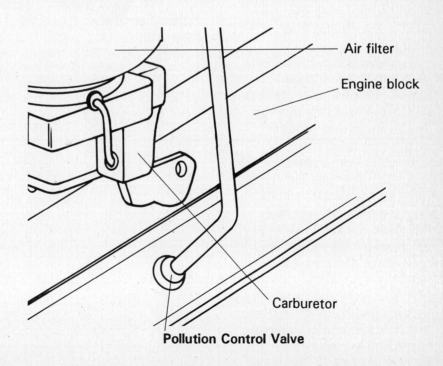

Air filter

Engine block

Carburetor

Pollution Control Valve

The Filters

Clean air, oil and fuel filters are vital to extend the life of your car. In addition to the dirt and other foreign matter which enter the engine and transmission from the outside, your car also creates its own contaminants through wear, condensation, and chemical reactions. Without filters, some components would not last more than a few miles.

The *air filter* is usually inside a large can or box on top of, or next to, the engine. It only takes a few minutes to inspect and replace the air filter. A clean filter protects the engine and allows it to operate at maximum efficiency. A conscientious owner can help the emission control system work properly and can maximize mileage with a few simple filter changes.

Here are some other filters you should know about: the *oil filter* and *the transmission filter* both trap dirt and metal filings and protect finely machined parts; the *crankcase vent or breather filter* which prevents dirt from entering crankcase; and the *fuel filter* which traps rust, sediment, dirt and other particles which may enter the carburetor and clog tiny fuel jets.

The *vapor canister* which returns gasoline vapors from the fuel system to the carburetor is also considered among your car's filters.

Changing and checking the vapor canister filters should be done by a mechanic.

The fuel filter removes dirt and other materials from the fuel before it reaches the sensitive carburetor or fuel injection components. The longer it does its job, the less able it is to remove dirt from the fuel. If the filter gets partially or completely clogged, the engine will run poorly or not at all. Therefore, it is important to change this filter every 12,000 miles. (See Chapter 7 for how to change the fuel filter.)

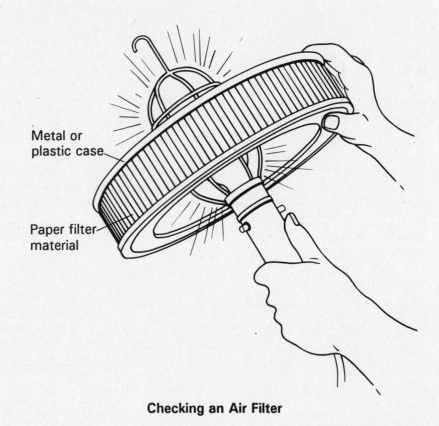

Metal or plastic case

Paper filter material

Checking an Air Filter

The Air Filter

Almost every vehicle has a replaceable air filter made with a ring of accordion-folded special filter paper. It traps dust, minute particles of sand, metal, glass and grit which would otherwise be drawn into the cylinders, where they would produce abrasion and premature wear.

You can usually tell the filter needs changing simply by looking at it. If it appears dirty, change it. If you are not sure how clean your filter is, try the following: When your engine has warmed up, put the car in park or neutral and, with the emergency brake on, let the car idle. Open the filter lid and remove the filter. If the engine begins to run faster, you need to change the filter. Another test is to remove the filter and rotate it around a light. You should see light through the entire rotation. If not, follow these directions to change the filter.

As it does its job trapping particles, the folds of the filter paper gradually become clogged, and as a result, engine vacuum does not draw in enough air. Too little air in the fuel/air mixture equals too much gasoline which in turn goes unburned. Economy and performance both suffer.

The filter should be changed every 12,000 miles under normal conditions.

Repair rating: Basic.

What you need: A tool to remove the air filter cover. If secured with one or two wing-nuts, your fingers will do it. Do not use pliers. Over the life of the car, these nuts will be removed many times; pliers make the nuts unusable.

Finally, you'll need the *exact* replacement filter. Use of an incorrect size or an inferior quality filter could void your warranty!

What to do:
1. Wipe off the air filter cover and surrounding area, so contaminants won't fall into the "throat" of the carburetor or throttle body.

2. Remove the filter cover. Because of gasket material ringing the edge, it may adhere a little more strongly than you think.

3. Remove the old filter.

4. Wipe out the filter holder, removing as much dust and oil as possible.

5. Put the new filter in place, being sure it's right side up.

6. Replace the filter cover and tighten down the mounting nuts or bolts.

Note: If the Breather Filter is inside the air cleaner cover, you should change it at the same time.

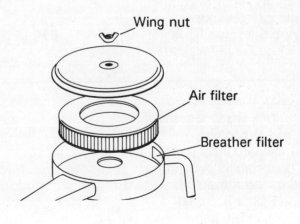

Air Filter

The Breather Filter

The breather filter is the air inlet to the PCV (Positive Crankcase Ventilation) system. It traps dirt and abrasive particles that would otherwise be sucked into the crankcase through the PCV valve. There are enormous varieties of styles, appearances, and locations of these filters. In a small number of cars, these filters are not replaceable and must be removed, cleaned, oiled, and then put back. Check with your dealer.

Repair rating: Basic.

What you need: The same tools required to remove the air filter cover will usually allow you to gain access to the breather filter. If you are replacing the filter element only (and not the housing and filter assembly) your fingers will do the job. Otherwise, you may need a screwdriver and needle-nosed and regular pliers.

What can go wrong: Breather filters are so familiar and part of such an old system, that they are often overlooked, occasionally even by professional technicians. If the breather filter is not noticed, and therefore not replaced, it can become clogged with contaminant particles plus oil and grease. The PCV valve produces a minutely metered and necessary volume of air to the intake manifold. If the breather filter is partially or fully clogged, the engine is starved for air, runs rich, wastes fuel, and produces poor performance and economy.

The breather filter should be changed every 10,000 to 12,000 miles, more often in dusty or severe conditions.

What to do:
1. Buy the exact replacement filter.

2. Remove the old breather filter by simply lifting it out with your fingers, and wipe the area clean.

3. Install the new one.

4. Tighten, replace, and secure any bolts, nuts, and clips that were removed to do the job.

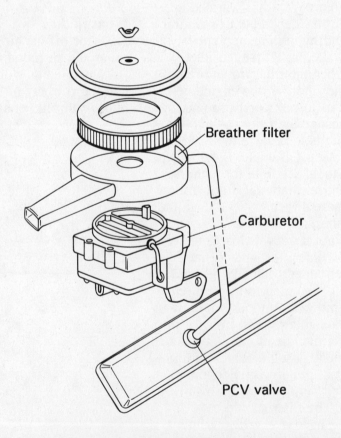

One Location of Breather Filter

In a national survey, automobile mechanics said drive belts and hoses were among the most neglected parts of the car. Due to the fact that these account for the majority of overheating problems, routinely replacing them after three to four years, can add to the life of your car *and* save an on the road breakdown.

The average engine has two or three belts. One belt drives the water pump, another drives the alternator or generator which charges the battery, and a third usually drives the air conditioning. These belts, which are called V-Belts because they are V-shaped rather than being flat or round, may also power the air conditioner's compressor or, occasionally, an emission control pump.

A drive belt is the same device that was once known as a "fan belt." It delivers engine power to one or more engine accessories, such as the cooling system fan, water pump, alternator, power steering pump, and air conditioner. Many vehicles use more than one belt, though to save space in late model small cars, a single "serpentine" belt is used to deliver power to all accessories. If yours is a multi-belt engine, it's wise to change all the belts at the same time. The innermost belt is the most difficult to reach and involves removing the outermost belts anyway.

Drive belt squeal and screech can be a cry for help. The belts may be to telling you that they have grown loose and flabby. When belts slip, they can overheat which may cause them to crack and break. If the belt breaks (or slips badly) you could be without power steering, a battery charger (alternator), or a functioning water pump.

You can save yourself heartache and sometimes a substantial amount of money avoiding a rip-off on parts like voltage regulators, alternators, and batteries simply by checking the drive belts. Many times, what appears to be serious electrical, cooling, or air conditioning problems are nothing more than a loose belt. Any one of these items could cause engine failure and result in a safety hazard.

Belt Problems

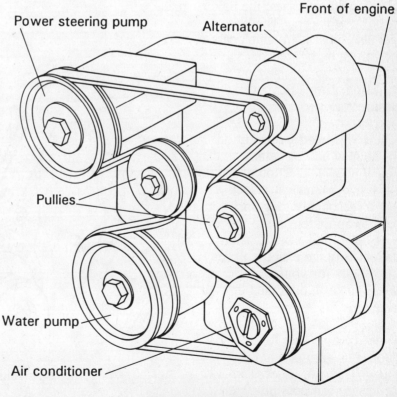

Power steering pump

Alternator

Front of engine

Pullies

Water pump

Air conditioner

A Complex Belt System

Repairing the Belts

Check the belts by pressing down on the middle of each belt. It shouldn't give more than about half an inch. If it does, it needs to be tightened. Check for wear and cracks.

To check the alternator-belt tension, grasp the vanes on the front of the alternator and try to turn them without using a lot of force. If they turn easily the belt is probably too loose and should be tightened.

What can go wrong: A belt rarely breaks. More often, the belt will fray, its reinforcing fibers will stretch and weaken, or its surface will become hard and "glazed." In any of these cases, the belt must be replaced. The belts can also loosen, in which case they must be tightened.

Repair rating: Beyond Basic.

What you need: In addition to the new belt or belts, you'll need a selection of the right size wrenches or sockets, a reasonably long "pry bar" to apply tension to the new belts, and a belt tension gauge. Buy the exact replacement belts for your specific year, make, model, and engine size.

What to do: Due to enormous variation among models, no single set of instructions can possibly refer to all situations. However, these general principles apply.

In the case of a serpentine belt, routing is critical, and it can be installed incorrectly. If you can't find the diagram for your engine, make a simple diagram before you remove the old belt.

1. Locate the adjusting strap. Slightly loosen both the mounting bolt and the adjusting bolt, but don't remove them. Push inward on the accessory, generally the alternator, to loosen the belt.

2. Remove the old belt, and install the new one in its place.

3. Using a prybar, and the help of a friend if available, to pry outward on the accessory, thereby tightening the belt. Caution: Never apply pressure on the aluminum or sheet metal parts. Look for castings, bolts, or steel parts.

4. Tighten the adjusting and mounting nuts, release the prybar, and check with a belt tension gage.

5. Use the belt tension gauge to make sure you didn't tighten the belt too much or too little, and adjust, if necessary.

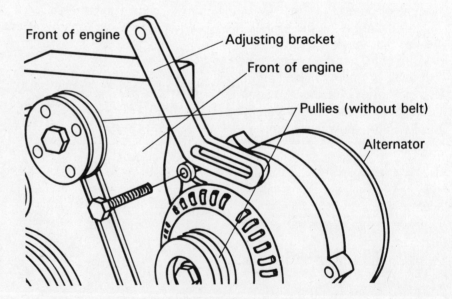

Belt Tensioning Bracket

5

There are a number of relatively easy repairs that you can do under the car, and often the most difficult part of the job is getting the repair. That's why many amateur mechanics let a problem under the car go unchecked. While repairs to many of the major mechanical items found under the car, such as the MacPherson strut suspension systems, springs, transmission, and complex brake work, are best left to the professionals, this chapter tells you what you can do--once you get there.

Because few of us have a gas station lift, repairing the systems under the car means jacking it up and supporting it. The most important advice is *be careful*. The process of jacking up and supporting a car is not that difficult. Accidents, however, are usually the result of not doing the job carefully.

In This Chapter...
The Suspension System   The Drive Line
The Braking System   The Exhaust System
The Tires

The Suspension System

The car's suspension system cushions the passengers and car from the many irregularities of the road. It also keeps the car from swaying back and forth when turning and from dipping up and down when starting and stopping. The front wheels of most cars are independently supported so that a bump on one side will not affect the other. Some cars also have independent rear suspension.

The suspension system is made up of springs, shock absorbers, the steering system, and various stabilizing bars, all of which combine so that you can effortlessly control a one-ton mass at speeds of up to 65 mph over various road conditions. Often, the various elements serve to control each other. The springs cushion the ride by allowing the car to move up and down, and the shocks absorb the up and down motion to prevent too bouncy a ride.

Support members are parts of the suspension system that support the weight of the vehicle. A MacPherson strut is a common support member, which became popular with the downsizing of automobiles. By combining the functions of several suspension pieces, the resulting assembly saves substantial weight. They are more commonly used on front suspensions, but they also appear on independent rear suspensions. One of the parts included in this assembly is the shock asorber.

Actual service of most suspension parts, with the exception of shock absorbers, is best left to professionals. There is considerable variation from one make and model of suspension piece to another, and most jobs require special tools.

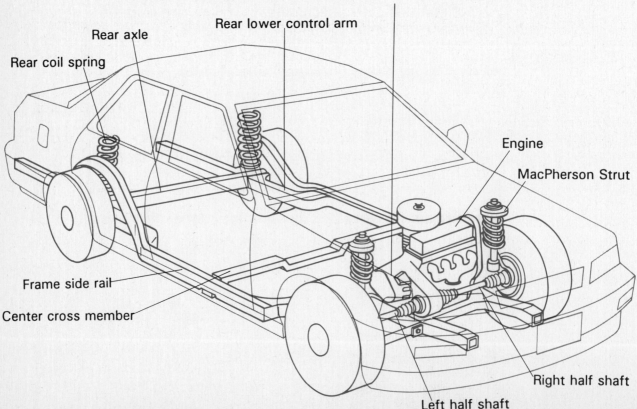

Transaxle assembly (combined transmission and drive axle)

Rear axle

Rear lower control arm

Rear coil spring

Engine

MacPherson Strut

Frame side rail

Center cross member

Right half shaft

Left half shaft

Front-wheel-drive, Transverse Front-Mounted Engine Chassis

Replacing Shock Absorbers

Your car's shock absorbers even out bumps from the road and keep the car from bouncing uncontrollably when a bump is encountered. Mounted between the suspension and the body, they not only smooth out the ride but they make steering steadier and safer. A shock absorber is one of the best known parts of the suspension system. Because of its difficult function, it's one of the most frequently replaced.

What can go wrong: Shock absorbers can leak, their connection to the car can break or become worn, or internal parts can fail. When a failure occurs you might hear grinding or clanking when you turn the wheel, or the car may simply bounce a great deal. In any case, this part loses its ability to absorb shocks.

Here's the test: At any corner of the car, start bouncing it. Once you get it going, quickly let go. A good shock will allow the car to bounce upward once only and then settle down. Continued bouncing indicates a bad shock at that corner. Repeat this test all around the car.

What you need: Your wrench and socket set is needed to remove the mounting hardware at the top and bottom of the shock absorber. Mountings vary from one model to another but are rarely complicated. A quick inspection will help you decide what few tools are needed. Especially on rear shocks, a pair of jackstands may be helpful. And, when you do the repair, save the nuts and bolts, because you will get some but not all new mounting hardware with your new shocks. *Remember, Never trust a bumper jack!*

If you often use your car for towing, you may decide to upgrade the original factory shocks with heavy duty ones. If so, be sure the parts store guarantees that they will fit and agrees to exchange them if they don't.

Repair rating: Basic

What to do:
1. Locate the front shocks by removing the top mounting bolts and hardware. They can be found almost directly over the wheels, but slightly inboard. Usually, there will be two bolts, but sometimes there will only be one. Make a diagram of the exact order in which nuts, washers, grommets, etc. are removed.

2. When the top of the shock is loose, push it as far downward as possible, using a hammer handle or a long screwdriver.

3. From beneath the car, remove the lower mounting bolts. Again, there are usually two. Make a diagram of the hardware you remove. Finish compressing the old shock absorber to its shortest possible length and work it free of the car.

4. Working with the bottom of the car, work the new shock into the same position that the old one occupied. Referring to your diagram, replace all mounting hardware, using as many new parts as possible. Tighten everything securely.

5. Before cleaning up, inspect the job to make sure your mounting matches the diagram that you made.

The Steering System

Many of today's cars come with some form of power steering mechanism. Power steering means that your steering wheel activates a booster to turn the wheels for you. This booster enables you to turn the wheels easily in low speed situations, such as parking.

The two aspects of your steering system most likely to cause problems are the connection of the steering system to the front wheels and the power steering mechanism. Over time, after hitting pot holes and curbs, the steering assembly around the front wheels will become loose. Your wheels may no longer be straight up and down, or they may "toe-in," where each of the front tires points slightly inward. The main problem with the power steering mechanism, which is hydraulic and needs fluid, is that the fluid can leak.

How to check it out: Unless the power steering system is leaking, fluid normally shouldn't have to be added. However, it's a good idea to check the fluid level every 6,000 miles or 6 months.

When a power steering system runs low on fluid, the pump will make a screeching noise. The steady, high-pitched sound will not be heard when the steering wheel is straight.

To make sure it is your steering system that is screeching, park the car with the engine running, and turn the steering wheel to one side and then to the other. If you hear the screech, your power steering reservoir is low, and the fluid needs to be checked. The noise occurs because air displaces the fluid, and the pump vibrates as it strikes the air.

What to do:
1. Check the power steering fluid with the engine at normal operating temperature, but not while it is running. The vehicle should be parked on a level surface with the front wheels pointed straight ahead. You can usually find the power steering pump, with its fluid reservoir, on the driver's side and connected to the engine by a drive belt.

Usually, a little dipstick is built right into the top of the cap. If not, you can tell where the fluid is from markings along the side of the reservoir neck. The fluid level should be maintained above the ADD mark on the reservoir.

On some vehicles the power steering reservoir is mounted away from the pump. The fluid level in these reservoirs can usually be checked without removing a cap or cover.

2. To add fluid, wipe the cap before removing it in order to prevent dirt from getting into the fluid. Then remove it.

3. Be sure you have the right fluid. In most cars, but not all, power steering fluid is the same as automotic transmission fluid.

4. Use a funnel to fill the reservoir to the indicated mark. Avoid over-filling.

5. Close the cap securely and start the engine. Purge the system by turning the steering wheel from full left to full right five to ten times with the engine running. Turn off the engine and recheck the level.

6. Check the fluid level every few days after adding to make sure that it's not leaking. If the level indicates a leak, check the hoses connected to the pump for leaks, wear, or chafing. If the hoses appear worn or cracked, they need to be replaced. Because of the high fluid pressures, repairing leaks or replacing hoses should be done by professionals only.

Alignment

Misalignment is a problem associated with your steering and suspension systems. Your first tip-offs to misalignment are uneven tire wear, poor handling, or both. Handling problems include the car's pulling to one side or another, failing to return properly to center after a turn, or shaking or vibration at certain speeds. You can often tell what type of alignment problem exists by looking at the tread wear pattern of the tires.

Once aligned, your wheels should stay that way for at least a year or more if the car has not been subjected to heavy impacts or accident damage.

A wheel alignment will correct most steering and handling problems unless the parts are badly worn, the tires are out of balance, or the shock absorbers are weak.

One important do-it-yourself steering and alignment check involves standing outside of your car with your wheels straight ahead. Reach inside the car and turn the steering wheel while you watch the tires. The tires should begin to move at the same time you move the wheel. If you notice any delay, have your steering checked out. You may have a loose or worn driving arm or idler arm in your steering linkage, which is an extremely dangerous condition.

Another check for misalignment is to let go of the steering wheel carefully, when it is safe to do so, and see if the car drifts to one side. If it does, you should have the alignment checked.

Proper alignment improves tire wear, steering, and fuel economy. A car with misaligned wheels has a higher rolling resistance and makes the engine work harder.

Chassis Lubrication

A large amount of movement takes place under your car that creates a great amount of friction. Friction creates heat and will wear down parts, thereby rendering them less fit to do their jobs. In order to reduce the wear on the parts, lubricants (usually some form of grease or oil) are applied to them to decrease the amount of friction.

Over time, the lubricants on these parts must be replenished. By applying these lubricants, a chassis lubrication (lube) keeps the parts on your car functioning properly.

Performing a chassis lubrication on one's own car is a labor of love. That's because there are so many shops that will do the job while you wait, for a very small fee. Specialty shops that offer nothing but oil changes and chassis lubes are everywhere. To meet competition from this source, new car dealers offer comparable, prompt service at reasonable prices.

Some cars today use a system of permanent lubrication on ball joints. Grease is injected into sealed areas around ball joints. These areas are protected from dirt, air, and water, and therefore they last pretty well and do not need to be lubricated.

Repair rating: Basic.

What you need: In order to perform a chassis lube yourself, you need to either buy, rent, or borrow a grease gun. These guns often have chambers for which replacement cartridges of lubricant are sold. You'll also need a can of spray lubricant, such as WD-40, a special lubricant for rubber parts, and the lubrication diagram for your particular make and model. Finally, you need a safe method of raising the car in order to work underneath it. A pair of ramps or safety jacks will do. Remember, *never trust a bumper jack*.

What to do:
1. A thorough chassis lubrication includes checking and topping off all fluids, including brake fluid, automatic transmission fluid, battery electrolyte, power steering fluid, clutch fluid if applicable, radiator coolant, windshield washer detergent, and any other fluids found under the hood.

2. All drive belts should be checked for wear and proper tension.

3. Brake lines, suspension parts, wiring, exhaust system, steering linkage, drive lines, and tires should all be carefully inspected.

4. Using your lubrication diagram, you must identify and carefully lubricate the many pieces of your suspension and steering systems under the car.

Doing a chassis lube occasionally can be satisfying, but with a power hoist and pressurized grease guns, a competent shop can do a thorough job at an economical price.

The Braking System

Your brake system uses the mechanical advantage of hydraulic pressure to allow you to stop a 3,000 pound object easily. That is why a relatively light touch of the foot can stop your car, even when it is going 55 mph.

Modern cars have two separate braking systems, each of which stops two wheels. Sometimes the systems are divided between the front and the rear; in other cars, they are divided diagonally.

In either case, the brake pedal operates a master cylinder, which is found under the hood on the driver's side. When the driver pushes the brake pedal, the master cylinder compresses the brake fluid. The pressure passes through the brake lines to actuating cylinders at each wheel. At the wheel, the pressure pushes brake shoes or pads to contact drums or rotors, and the friction stops the car. Drum brakes force the brake pads against the inside of a revolving drum, creating friction to slow down the car. Disc brakes work much like bicycle brakes, with the pads squeezing together around a spinning disc.

What can go wrong: Brake systems can fail either because the fluid in the brake lines has leaked out or because the pads are worn out.

In addition, trouble can begin when air gets into the brake lines. You may experience this problem if the fluid level is too low in the reservoir above the master cylinder. Brake fluid is not easily compressible, so it maintains a constant pressure in the brake lines. Air is readily compressible, and if it is in the brake lines, it absorbs pressure that the brake fluid would not. The result is spongy and unreliable brakes.

While your brakes are the most important safety item on the car, they are often the most ignored. A simple test will signal problems. If you have power brakes, turn on the engine to do the test. Push the brake pedal down and hold it down. The pedal should stop firmly about halfway to the floor and stay there. If the pedal has a mushy feel or keeps moving slowly to the floor, you should have your brakes checked.

If you have built-in brake wear indicators, you'll hear a high-pitched squealing or cricket-like warning sound when it's time for new brake linings. The sound may come and go, or you may hear it whenever the wheels are rolling. It usually stops when the brake pedal is pushed down firmly. Some cars even have a dashboard warning light, indicating when your brakes

need new linings or pads.

As brake linings wear, you will have to push the pedal farther to slow the car. However, if you have automatic adjusters, they'll take up the slack and maintain proper pedal travel. Brake linings will finally wear out from slowing and stopping thousands of times. When that happens, get a qualified service center to replace the necessary parts. And make sure they check the master cylinder, wheel cylinders, and all other components of the system. They may also be due for service when the linings are replaced.

There are good reasons why you should leave extensive brake work to your mechanic. In addition to the dangers of working with asbestos, procedures such as checking caliper pistons, turning the rotor in a brake lathe, or sanding the pads are usually too complicated for a do-it-yourselfer. In the end, very little money will be saved by doing brake work yourself.

Parking brakes let you know when they need adjustment. As linings wear, you must move the handle or foot pedal a greater distance before the brakes fully apply. The cables and linkage should be lubricated when the parking brakes are adjusted.

Checking Your Brake Fluid

The most important item in brake system maintenance is periodic checking of the brake fluid level. Check the level at least at every oil change. Many new cars have transluscent brake fluid reservoirs in which the level can be checked without removing the cover.

On cars with opaque reservoirs, carefully wipe off the reservoir cover to remove any dirt before checking the level. Then pry the retaining clip aside and remove the cover. The fluid level should be kept about 1/2-inch from the top on reservoirs that are not otherwise marked.

If you add your own brake fluid, buy it in small cans and store them, tightly sealed, in a cool, dry place. Discard open containers after one year. Brake fluid absorbs moisture, and excess moisture can damage your brake system.

Three different grades of automotive brake fluid are available. Using the correct grade is essential in order to maintain proper brake operation in all driving conditions. Check your owner's manual for the right brake fluid for your car. Also, be careful not to spill brake fluid on painted surfaces. Some grades contain a paint solvent and will quickly strip finished surfaces.

It is normal for the brake fluid level to go down over a long period of time. However, if brake fluid must be frequently added, there may be a leak in the system. Have the brakes checked by a professional.

The color of your brake fluid can also indicate trouble. The fluid should not appear overly dark. If it does, it's probably old and overdue for replacement. Brake fluid deteriorates with age and will absorb water from the atmosphere. This could cause old fluid to boil in hard use, causing your brakes to fail. Old fluid can also cause the metal parts in your brake system to corrode and wear faster.

Some car makers recommend changing the brake fluid every 24 months, regardless of mileage. This preventative maintenance can increase the life of any car's brake system but should be performed by a professional technician.

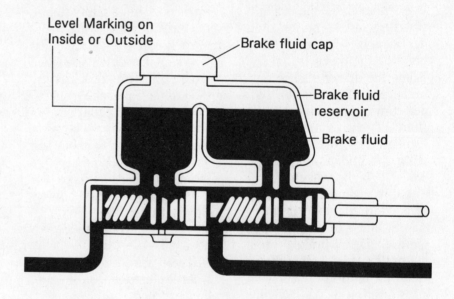

Level Marking on Inside or Outside

Brake fluid cap

Brake fluid reservoir

Brake fluid

Changing Your Brake Fluid

The Tires

The tire has to perform more simultaneous functions than any other part of a car, including bearing the load, steering, cushioning the ride, moving the car, and stopping.

Tire pressure is one of the most ignored items of auto maintenance, despite the fact that it affects three different areas of auto operation: tire wear, fuel consumption, and vehicle handling. Gasoline mileage can drop as much as 0.5 percent for every one pound per square inch (psi) of under-inflation. Under-inflation of the tire by 4 psi can reduce a tire's life by 10 percent. Inadequate tire pressure can also make the vehicle unsafe to drive.

Types of Tires: There are three types of tires on the market today: bias ply, belted bias, and radial.

Bias ply tires are made with layers (or plies) of cords which criss-cross each other. These cords may be arranged in two or more (even numbered) layers. The more layers, the stronger the tire.

Belted bias tires have cords arranged in a criss-cross pattern (like bias ply) as well as two or more layers of fabric or steel "belts" over the cords. These belts increase the overall strength of the tire. Belted tires tend to run cooler and last longer than bias ply tires.

Radial tires are provided on all new cars sold in the U.S. The cords in a radial tire run at right angles to the center line and may be in one to three layers (plies). Over this radial section is added a 4 ply belt, with cords that run at a slight angle to the center line of the tire. The result is a tire with a flexible sidewall (that's why radials often look like they need air), but with stiffness and strength in the tread. These characteristics add up to longer tread life and improved fuel efficiency.

Warning: Never mix radials with other tire types.

Buying Tires: If you need new tires, radials can improve your mileage from 3 to 7 percent over conventional bias ply tires. They also last longer and usually improve the way your car handles.

Snow and all-season are two subcategories of tires. Snow tires have an open tread pattern with deep grooves. Because snow tires wear out rapidly on dry roads and are inconvenient to change, the all-season tire has become one of the more popular tires on the market. The all-season-tread pattern is effective in occasional snow, has good traction on wet roads, and will last longer than snow tires on dry roads.

Retreads are another option when buying tires. In building a tire, adding the tread is the last step of the process. A retreader takes undamaged tires, strips off the remaining tread, and repeats the last step of the original manufacturing process. Retreads can save 30 to 50 percent over the price of a similar new tire, and high quality retreads will perform nearly as well. The National Tire Dealers and Retreaders Association (NTDRA) rates retread plants on a scale of A to F. A and B are passing, with A the best. When buying a retread, be sure to ask for the manufacturer's NTDRA rating. Buying an A rated retread is an excellent way to save money, especially on a vehicle used mostly for short trips or stop-and-go driving.

Tire grades: To help consumers compare tires, the government now requires tires to have mileage and safety ratings. This little-known system grades tires according to treadwear, traction, and heat resistance. These grades are printed on the sidewall and attached to the tire on a paper label. In addition, every dealer can provide you with the grades of the tires the store sells.

The system works like this: The treadwear grade gives you an idea of how much mileage to expect from a tire. It is shown in numbers: 90, 100, 110, 120, and so forth. A tire graded 150 should give you 50 percent more mileage than one graded 100. In order to *estimate* the expected mileage, multiply the treadwear grade by 200. Under average conditions, a tire graded 150 (times 200) should last 30,000 miles. Because individual driving habits vary considerably, it is best to use the treadwear as a relative basis of comparison, rather than an absolute predictor of mileage.

For most of us, high mileage is the most important aspect of a tire. However, few of us realize that where we live is a key factor in determining how long tires will last. In addition to construction and design, tire wear is affected by the level of abrasive material used in road surfaces. Generally, the West Coast, Great Lakes region, and northern New England have road surfaces that are easiest on tires. The Appalachian and Rocky Mountain areas are hardest on tires.

Traction is graded A, B, and C and describes the tire's ability to stop on wet surfaces. Tires graded A will stop on a wet road in a shorter distance than tires graded B or C. Tires rated C have poor traction. If you often drive on wet roads, buy a tire with a high traction grade.

Heat resistance is also graded A, B, and C. This grading is important, because hot-running tires can result in blowouts or tread separation. An A rating means the tire will run cooler than one rated B or C and is less likely to fail if driven over long distances at highway speeds. In addition, tires that run cooler tend to be more fuel efficient. If you often drive at high speed, a high heat resistance grade is best.

The tables on the following pages list the top rated tires and their grades. In addition, you'll find an indication of their expected mileage.

Tire Gauge

Studies show that gauges built into air pumps at service stations are generally wrong. Having a reliable tire gauge is a must if you're filling up your own tires. One of the best we've found is also one of the least expensive and comes with some very useful information about tire care. For a handy and accurate tire pressure gauge, send $4.00 to the Tire Industry Safety Council, Box 1801, Washington, D.C. 20013, and ask for their gauge and tire care kit.

Tire Grades

Top Rated Radials

Brand Name	Model	Description	Grades			Expected Mileage		
			Trac.	Heat	Tred.	High	Medium	Low
General	Ameri Classic	15	A	B	400	120,000	80,000	60,000
Vogue	CBR Touring	P205, P215/70R15	A	B	400	120,000	80,000	60,000
Vogue	CBR VI	All	A	B	400	120,000	80,000	60,000
Armstrong	Five Star	15	A	B	370	111,000	74,000	55,500
Big-O	Legacy	15	A	B	370	111,000	74,000	55,500
Continental	CS24	15	A	B	370	111,000	74,000	55,500
Dunlop	Elite	All	A	B	370	111,000	74,000	55,500
Kelly	Voyager 1000	All	A	B	370	111,000	74,000	55,500
Montgomery Ward	Road Tamer 900	15 Except	A	B	370	111,000	74,000	55,500
Medalist	Defender 70	P185-P205/70R14	A	C	370	111,000	74,000	55,500
Arizonian	Silver Edition	14&15	A	B	360	108,000	72,000	54,000
Centennial	Constitution	All	A	B	360	108,000	72,000	54,000
Cordovan	Grand Prix SE	All	A	B	360	108,000	72,000	54,000
Cordovan	Wild Trac RTV	All	A	B	360	108,000	72,000	54,000
Douglas	Premium	14&15	A	B	360	108,000	72,000	54,000
Hallmark	Trail Buster	All	A	B	360	108,000	72,000	54,000
Jetzon	Grandeur	14&15	A	B	360	108,000	72,000	54,000
Kelly	Safari AWR	All	A	B	360	108,000	72,000	54,000
Lee	GT V Trak	14&15	A	B	360	108,000	72,000	54,000
Monarch	Ultra STL Trac	14&15	A	B	360	108,000	72,000	54,000
Multi-Mile	Wild Ctry RVT	All	A	B	360	108,000	72,000	54,000
Remington	Society	All	A	B	360	108,000	72,000	54,000
Safemark	SBR IV	14&15	A	B	360	108,000	72,000	54,000
Shell	2000	14&15	A	B	360	108,000	72,000	54,000
Sigma	Grand Sport Stampede	All	A	B	360	108,000	72,000	54,000
Star	Trail Buster APR	All	A	B	360	108,000	72,000	54,000
Winston	Fun & Mud	All	A	B	360	108,000	72,000	54,000
Hallmark	Ultimate PSR	14&15	A	C	360	108,000	72,000	54,000
Kumho	Centurion	14&15	A	C	360	108,000	72,000	54,000
Medalist	SX5000 SR	15	A	C	360	108,000	72,000	54,000
Star	Centurion PSR	14&15	A	C	360	108,000	72,000	54,000
Winston	Signature SR	All	A	C	360	108,000	72,000	54,000
Cornell	1000	14&15	B	B	360	108,000	72,000	54,000
Armstrong	Five Star	14	A	B	350	105,000	70,000	52,500
Atlas	Pinnacle SE 70	All	A	B	350	105,000	70,000	52,500
Big-O	Legacy	P205/75R15	A	B	350	105,000	70,000	52,500
Big-O	Legacy	14	A	B	350	105,000	70,000	52,500
Continental	CS24	14	A	B	350	105,000	70,000	52,500
Cooper	Lifeliner SR	All	A	B	350	105,000	70,000	52,500
Cornell	Futura XWT	All	A	B	350	105,000	70,000	52,500
Dayton	Triple Crown SL	All	A	B	350	105,000	70,000	52,500
Dean	Quasar	All	A	B	350	105,000	70,000	52,500
Duralon	IV Plus	All	A	B	350	105,000	70,000	52,500
El Dorado	Crusader	All	A	B	350	105,000	70,000	52,500
Exxon	Signature II, 70	All	A	B	350	105,000	70,000	52,500
Falls	Mastercraft SR	All	A	B	350	105,000	70,000	52,500
General	Ameri Classic	14	A	B	350	105,000	70,000	52,500
General	Ameri Tech St	All	A	B	350	105,000	70,000	52,500
Gillette	Kodiak+4 80	14&15	A	B	350	105,000	70,000	52,500
Hercules	Ultra Plus	All	A	B	350	105,000	70,000	52,500
Mohawk	Millennium	14&15	A	B	350	105,000	70,000	52,500

Tire Grades

Top Rated Radials

Brand Name	Model	Description	Grades			Expected Mileage		
			Trac.	Heat	Tred.	High	Medium	Low
Montgomery Ward	Road Tamer 900	P205/75R15	A	B	350	105,000	70,000	52,500
Montgomery Ward	Road Tamer 900	14	A	B	350	105,000	70,000	52,500
Panther	Premier 70	All	A	B	350	105,000	70,000	52,500
Peerless	Permasteel+4 80	14&15	A	B	350	105,000	70,000	52,500
Road King	RK SL	All	A	B	350	105,000	70,000	52,500
Sigma	Supreme 70SE	All	A	B	350	105,000	70,000	52,500
Starfire	Spectrum SRW	All	A	B	350	105,000	70,000	52,500
Vogue	CBR Touring	P215/65R15	A	B	350	105,000	70,000	52,500
Medalist	Defender 70	14&15	A	C	350	105,000	70,000	52,500
Medalist	SX5000 SR	14	A	C	350	105,000	70,000	52,500
Cooper	Lifeliner	14&15	B	C	350	105,000	70,000	52,500
Dean	AST Steel	14&15	B	C	350	105,000	70,000	52,500
El Dorado	Odyssey	14&15	B	C	350	105,000	70,000	52,500
Falls	Mastercraft	14&15	B	C	350	105,000	70,000	52,500
Hercules	Ultrapreme	14&15	B	C	350	105,000	70,000	52,500
Sigma	Supreme 80SE 75SE	14&15	B	C	350	105,000	70,000	52,500
Starfire	Spectrum	14&15	B	C	350	105,000	70,000	52,500
Goodrich	Comp HR4	All Others	A	A	340	102,000	68,000	51,000
Goodrich	Comp VR4	All	A	A	340	102,000	68,000	51,000
Dayton	S/R	13	A	B	340	102,000	68,000	51,000
Gillette	Sprint G/T	13	A	B	340	102,000	68,000	51,000
Goodyear	Double Eagle	All	A	B	340	102,000	68,000	51,000
Goodyear	Invicta GS	All Others	A	B	340	102,000	68,000	51,000
Panther	Eclipse	13	A	B	340	102,000	68,000	51,000
Road King	Widetrack S/R	13	A	B	340	102,000	68,000	51,000
Winston	Classic	14&15	A	B	340	102,000	68,000	51,000
Medalist	Defender 60	P255-P275/60R15	A	C	340	102,000	68,000	51,000
Cordovan	Classic Premium	All	B	C	340	102,000	68,000	51,000
Multi-Mile	Classic Premium	All	B	C	340	102,000	68,000	51,000
Sigma	Classic Premium	All	B	C	340	102,000	68,000	51,000
Armstrong	Five Star	13	A	B	330	99,000	66,000	49,500
Firestone	FR480	All	A	B	330	99,000	66,000	49,500
General	Ameri Classic	13	A	B	330	99,000	66,000	49,500
Michelin	XH,HW4	All	A	B	330	99,000	66,000	49,500
Mohawk	Millennium	13	A	B	330	99,000	66,000	49,500
Sumitomo	SC660	All	Trac.	B	330	99,000	66,000	49,500
Medalist	Defender 60	P235-P245/60R15	A	C	330	99,000	66,000	49,500
Medalist	Defender 60	P235-P245/60R14	A	C	330	99,000	66,000	49,500
Medalist	Defender 70	13	A	C	330	99,000	66,000	49,500
Riken	Classic STX-70	14&15	A	A	320	96,000	64,000	48,000
Arizonian	Silver Edition	13	A	B	320	96,000	64,000	48,000
Big-O	Legacy	13	A	B	320	96,000	64,000	48,000
Continental	CS24	13	A	B	320	96,000	64,000	48,000
Cornell	1000	13	A	B	320	96,000	64,000	48,000
Dayton	S/R	15	A	B	320	96,000	64,000	48,000
Douglas	Premium	13	A	B	320	96,000	64,000	48,000
Gillette	Sprint G/T	15	A	B	320	96,000	64,000	48,000
Goodyear	Invicta GS	13	A	B	320	96,000	64,000	48,000
Lee	GT V Trak	13	A	B	320	96,000	64,000	48,000
Monarch	Ultra STL Trac	13	A	B	320	96,000	64,000	48,000
Montgomery Ward	Road Tamer 700	14&15	A	B	320	96,000	64,000	48,000

When you insert the top of a penny into a tread groove, if any part of Lincoln's head is visible, it's time to replace the tire. While this old rule of thumb is still valid, today's tires have a built in wear indicator. A series of smooth horizontal wear bars will appear across the surface of your tire when the tread depth reaches the danger zone.

Your tires tread can tell you a great deal about how well you are taking care of them, and they can even provide important information about your suspension system. The following list shows some typical signals your tires may be giving you and their probable cause.

If you see:

o   Wear on the sides of the tread, the tire is underinflated.

o Wear in the middle of the tread, the tire is overinflated.

o Random patches of wear, the tire is out of balance or the wheel rim may be bent.

o Wear on one shoulder, you may have a wheel alignment problem.

o   Circular wear spots, you may have faulty shock absorbers.

o   Wear in a random pattern, the wheel chamber needs adjusting or the wheel toe-in setting is incorrect.

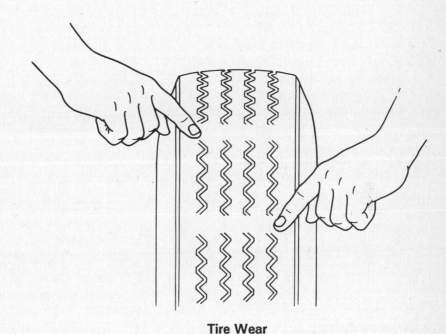

Tire Wear

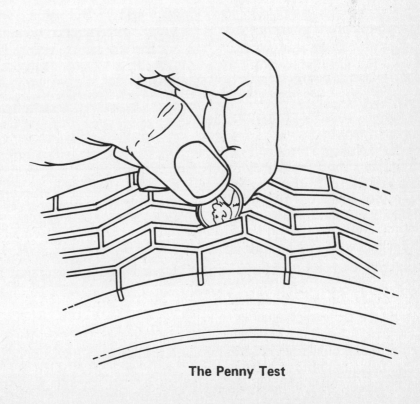

The Penny Test

Rotating Your Tires

Because tires wear differently according to where they are on the car, you can extend the life of your tires by rotating them on a regular basis. A car handles better when tire tread patterns are evenly worn. Also, when the tires wear out, it may be possible to buy a set of four more economically than two pairs at different times.

Some cars have a dashboard signal, indicating that it is time to rotate the tires. Otherwise a good rule of thumb is to rotate them every 10,000 miles. No matter what kind of tires you have, rotating them regularly will add miles to their life.

The recommended rotation pattern for all vehicles with radial tires is to move the two front tires to the rear, same side, and then the rear tires to the front, same side. The spare can be included in the rotation on cars with conventional spare tires.

Repair shops can lift all four wheels off the ground and rotate your tires in a matter of minutes for just a few dollars. They'll know the proper rotation pattern, and they will inspect your tires as they do the work.

However, you can do this relatively simple job yourself. With the car parked on a level surface, the parking brake engaged, and blocks set in front and behind the tires not being worked on, back off each lug nut on the tire you are removing about a quarter turn before you jack up the car. You should never trust a bumper jack, so use it only to raise the car, and then set the car down on safety jack stands available at any parts store. To rotate tires, you will need at least two jack stands, and if you have four, the job will go even quicker. Then follow the appropriate rotation pattern and the following directions for changing a tire.

Patching a Tire

Patching a tire is not recommended for a do-it-yourselfer.

When a modern tire, especially a steel-belted radial tire, suffers a puncture, safe practice demands that the tire be dismounted (removed from the wheel) and carefully inspected for concealed damage. Any tire shop has the power equipment to do this check in a matter of minutes at very low cost. Don't forget to ask the price before you authorize the work.

If the tire is not reparable, riding on it could endanger your safety. If there is an easily fixable puncture, you'll want a patch applied on the inside of the tire and then vulcanized (heat cured) in place. This procedure requires that the tire be rebalanced after it is remounted on the wheel.

Changing a Tire

What can go wrong: A tire may develop a leak, and, as a result, lose air pressure and "go flat;" it may also blow out (deflate suddenly and explosively) as a result of a road hazard or vandalism.

Repair rating: Basic.

What you need: An appropriate jack is needed to lift the weight of the car. You also need a screwdriver or lever to remove the decorative hubcap, and a "lug wrench" to remove the tire mounting nuts, which are also referred to as "lug nuts." All of these items will come with your car. In your kit will also be one of two types of jacks--a scissors type, which you can use a screw mechanism to operate, and a lever type, which is on a square pole. Absolutely essential is a good spare tire. Your spare may be a temporary spare; it will look much smaller than your regular tires.

What to do:
1. Move the car to a safe place, as far away from the flow of traffic as possible. Set the parking brake, and be sure the transmission is in park if automatic or in low gear if manual. Block the wheel diagonally opposite the one you will be changing. Use a brick, a timber, a large rock, or a wedge of some kind, both in front of and behind the wheel you block.

2. Remove the spare tire from its compartment and position it near the defective tire.

3. Place the jack in position, and collect the rest of your tools. With a bumper jack, there will often be a "locating" hole on the under side of the bumper into which a tab from the jack will fit. With a "scissors" jack, there may be a similar hole or groove into which the jack fits, or there may simply be a "lifting pad" beneath the body. Your owner's manual will tell you exactly where to place the jack.

4. Remove the decorative hubcap if there is one. Usually these just pry off, but sometimes they are held in place with bolts.

5. With the full weight of the car still on the bad tire, use the lug wrench to loosen each mounting nut no more than half a turn.

6. Jack up the car. The spare may take up more room than the flat tire, so raise the car enough to allow extra space. The last thing you'd want would be to have to raise the car an extra inch with no tire on the wheel.

7. Use the lug wrench to loosen and remove the mounting nuts. Remove those at the top of the wheel last. Gravity will help hold the tire in place if the bottom nuts are removed first. Store the lug nuts inside the hubcap.

8. Remove the tire and wheel assembly, and drop it safely out of your way. Don't put it away yet.

9. Position the spare tire on the wheel lugs. Install the lug nuts "finger tight," starting with the topmost one. With the lug wrench, cinch them down safely, but not completely tight. If you have a collapsed-type spare, inflate it now.

10. Lower the car, and remove and stow the jack. Fully tighten the lug nuts.

11. Stow the flat tire, the lug wrench, and the blanket. Don't worry about the hubcap now; the shop that repairs your flat will replace it.

The Drive Line

Rear-drive cars: The drive line in a rear-drive automobile is the device that transmits power from the engine assembly to the rear axle. It lies centered under the car, begins at the rear of the transmission, whether manual or automatic, and extends to the differential.

The diameter of the drive line depends on the power of the engine in the car. The larger the engine, the stronger the drive line must be to deliver power without twisting. A typical diameter in a full-sized car with a 5000-cc (5.0 liter) engine would be about 3 inches.

The drive line is normally in two or more sections, separated by universal joints (U-joints) or constant velocity (CV) joints. CV joints consist of two universal joints close together, with a yoke between them; they can deliver more power through a sharper bend, with less vibration. Both U-joints and CV joints allow the shaft to "bend" around structural or other elements under the car.

What can go wrong: Drive lines are carefully balanced on special equipment to prevent vibration. Small steel weights are welded on in appropriate positions. Occasionally, a weight will fly off. More often, a large rock will dent or distort the drive line.

This produces some of the most elusive and annoying vibration an automobile owner can experience! It can masquerade as tires that are defective or out of balance, suspension that is out of alignment, bad shocks or struts, or worn wheel bearings. The source of the vibration can seem to come from anywhere. If you experience unexplainable vibration in a vehicle, a test drive by a thoroughly experienced professional is your best bet.

What to do: Regular lubrication of the U-joints is desirable, certainly at every chassis lube, and all good shops do this job.

A commom problem is that many cars leave the factory with no grease fittings, on the grounds that they contain "lifetime" lubrication. Omitting the grease fittings can save the factory 60 cents per car. Their estimate of a lifetime may differ from yours. Very rarely can these grease fittings be retrofitted into U-joints. Whenever yours wears out, be sure the replacements are not factory parts. Have your technician install a quality aftermarket brand that includes grease fittings.

Front-drive cars: In front drive cars, the drive lines are much shorter and somewhat more complex. The transmission, differential, and rear axle are replaced by a compact device known as a transaxle. This mechanism accepts power from the engine and performs all the functions of the transmission in controlling the ratio of drive-wheel rotation to engine speed. It then changes the direction of the power, as a differential does, and delivers power to both front wheels, usually using a CV joint on each side.

The CV joints and their associated splines are often covered by neoprene boots, which are cylinders that wrap around the assembly to protect the components from the dirt, grease, oil, fumes, and dust of the hostile environment under the hood. Due to wear and tear or mishap, these boots must be replaced fairly frequently. Factory recommended procedure is usually the time-consuming and costly approach of loosening each drive shaft at each wheel, sliding off the old boot, or "sleeve," and sliding on the new one. The aftermarket has developed split boots, which go on in two pieces, securely fastened together. Split boots are now in their second or third generation of engineering; they're excellent, and their installation costs much less. Note: If you're ever told you need new CV boots, insist on split boots!

Exhaust System

The exhaust system of any motor vehicle carries the burned gases produced by the engine to a safe location away from the driver. Generally, this safe spot is toward the rear of the car.

A typical exhaust system consists of one or more exhaust manifolds (the devices that accept exhaust from each cylinder and deliver it to a common point attached to the exhaust pipe), a cross pipe, an exhaust pipe, a muffler, a connecting pipe, a catalytic converter, another connecting pipe, a resonator, and a tail pipe. Most systems do not have all of these items; however, some cars have dual systems with two of everything.

The exhaust manifold collects burned gases from the individual cylinders and directs them to the exhaust pipe. Sometimes the exhaust manifold is an integral part of the cylinder head.

The exhaust pipe carries the gases to the muffler, which reduces noise by passing the hot gases over perforated baffles, reversing direction twice, and dissipating noise energy.

The catalytic converter passes the exhaust over heated beds of precious metal catalysts, usually platinum. This process converts the poisonous and noxious carbon monoxide into harmless carbon dioxide. The catalytic converter becomes very hot,

which is why you need to be careful when you park on tall, dry grass and leaves.

The resonator, a smaller muffler, further eliminates exhaust noise, particularly in the higher frequencies.

The tail pipe is the final element. It directs gases downward at the rear of the car, feeding out from the converter or resonator

The cross pipe, if there is one, carries exhaust gases from one side of a V-4, V-6, or V-8 engine to the exhaust pipe common point on the other side.

The connecting pipes join the muffler to the catalytic converter and the catalytic converter to the resonator.

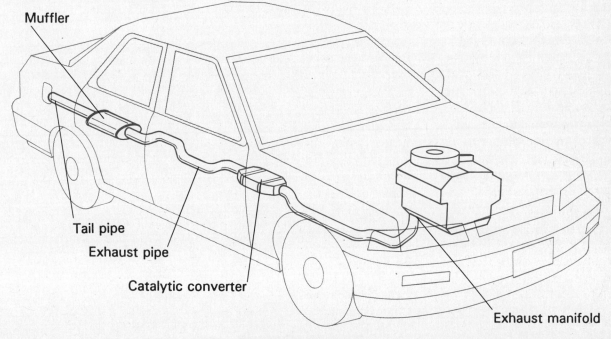

Muffler

Tail pipe

Exhaust pipe

Catalytic converter

Exhaust manifold

The Exhaust System

Owner service: The various sections of the exhaust system are welded together, which does not lend itself to easy do-it-yourself service. The owner should be observant for exhaust leaks, noises, or fumes. *These can be deadly.* Carbon monoxide can dull the driver's senses and make the driver perform worse than a legally drunk driver. If you smell exhaust, have your system checked and serviced. Your dealer or a local independent shop can do the work so inexpensively that it's hardly worth your time to try it yourself. Furthermore, repairing the exhaust system can be dangerous, largely because the system is under the car and parts must be removed with a cutting torch or a heavy hacksaw.

Buyer alert: Especially at chain or franchise operations, be certain you get a written estimate and that the estimate is complete and all-inclusive. Assure the manager that you will not pay one cent more than the written estimate. Shop around, and get at least three estimates.

Patching Holes in a Muffler

Using mending tape to patch a hole in a muffler would be a good idea only if you were preparing the vehicle for the short ride to the wrecking yard! If the muffler is old enough that is has blown a hole in its surface, it may have blown the hole to make a new path for the exhaust gases, which would otherwise be blocked inside. Patching the muffler creates excessively high exhaust backpressure, with a resulting severe loss of engine power.

Danger of carbon monoxide from a leaking exhaust system is too great. If your muffler is bad, have a professional replace it.

6

Your car's the electrical system has two main jobs: to start your car and keep it running and to provide electricity to run your lights, radio, and other electrical accessories.

Your car's battery provides the electricity for the starter motor and spark plugs by storing electricity produced by the alternator. When you turn the key, electricity from the battery passes through a coil, which increases its voltage. Then it goes to the distributor, which sends bursts of electricity to the spark plugs, igniting the fuel and powering the engine. Once the engine has started, electricity is provided by the alternator, which is driven by a belt connected to the engine. Thus, your engine becomes an electrical power generator. The battery is also recharged by the alternator while the engine is running. A voltage regulator ensures that the battery isn't damaged by overcharging.

Thus, your car is a self-contained electrical power plant. The primary purpose of the battery is to to start the engine. Once the engine is started, your car will run even if your battery is dead.

In This Chapter...

The Battery

Your car's battery stores the electricity that starts the car. It provides electrical current to the starter motor, which moves the pistons so that they build pressure At the same time, the battery supplies current to the spark plugs, in order to ignite the mixture of air and fuel that powers the car. It's a big job, requiring a lot of power over a short period of time. If your engine doesn't start right away, your battery must be strong enough to keep the electrical power up each time you try.

The battery has two terminals attached to either its top or its side; one is positive, the other negative. Most cars are "negative ground." This term means that the wire from the postive terminal powers the ignition system and other electrical components, and the wire from the negative terminal attaches to the car's frame in order to ground it.

Fluid level: Your battery requires a suffcent amount of electrolyte which is a mixture of water and sulfuric acid. If your battery has caps on the top, lift off the caps and check whether the fluid comes up to the bottom of the filler neck. Check this level once a month.

If the fluid level is low, add only distilled water, because minerals in tap water can contaminate your battery. If the temperature is below freez-ing, add water only if you plan to drive the car immediately. Newly added water can freeze and damage your battery.

Some batteries look sealed, with a single cap over three cells. Fluid level *must* be checked regularly, even in these batteries.

What can go wrong: Over time, temperature, use, and recharging cause a battery to wear out, and it loses its ability to store electricity. With proper care, however, a battery will easily last five to six years. Since cold air temperatures affect your battery, it may seem sluggish in the winter. Sometimes it may not be recharged properly due to a failure of the alternator. Dirty connections can prevent power from getting out, so they may cause your battery to appear to be dead. Battery failure can also be due to low fluid level.

Sometimes a dead battery that is dead will start immediately if you "jump" it.

The following pages include key battery checks and repairs, as well as directions for replacing your battery.

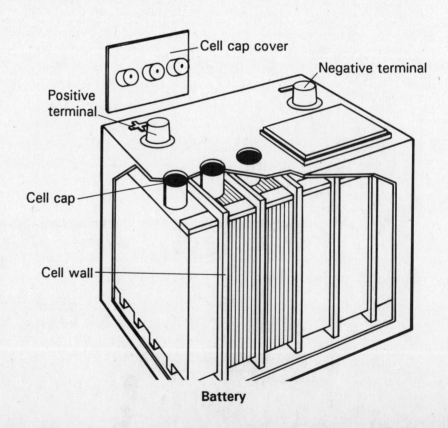

Battery

What NOT to Do Around Your Battery

Since we constantly use batteries in appliances around the house, our familiarity with them may breed a false sense of confidence about handling the battery in a car. In reality, that innocent-looking car battery can be the cause of serious injuries.

A car battery uses chemicals to produce electrical energy, and in so doing, it creates flammable and explosive hydrogen gas. A lit cigarette or spark can cause the hydrogen gas to explode. The following tips will help you prevent injury while you are working around the battery:

1. Never use a match or cigarette lighter to illuminate what you are doing, and never smoke near the battery.

2. Don't lean over the battery when working on it.

3. Whenever you work with the battery, always remove the negative (or ground) cable first; it is usually marked with a "minus" sign. When you are done, reconnect it last. This caution will greatly reduce the chance of causing a spark, which could ignite the hydrogen gas.

4. When using jumper cables, never connect the ground jumper cable to the negative post of the run down battery. Instead, connect it to the frame or the engine block of the stalled car, as far as possible from the battery.

5. Be careful when using tools around the battery. You could accidentally make a direct connection across the terminals or from the hot terminal to a grounded part of the car, creating a dangerous spark.

6. Don't allow battery electrolyte (acid) to contact skin, eyes, clothing, or paint.

7. If you are using a battery charger, make sure you hook it up correctly. Follow the directions on the charger, and be sure the charger is turned off or unplugged before making connections. Also, remember to turn the charger off and unplug it after charging and before disconnecting the charger leads.

8. Never use baking soda solutions to clean your battery. Baking soda is an alkali that, when mixed with the sulphuric acid in your battery, can produce a violent chemical reaction. This reaction could damage your battery and cause personal injury.

Cleaning the Battery Terminals and Cables

The battery cables carry the electrical current that powers the starter and other electrical components of the car.

What can go wrong: If your battery fails to start the engine, first check the battery cables. A common mistake is to buy a new battery when all that is really needed is a cleaning or a new set of cables. Look for frayed or cracked cables, and check for white, dusty corrosion around the connections. Corrosion around the battery connections can prevent electrical circuits from being completed, so electricity can not recharge the battery, and you may assume your perfectly good battery is "dead." Corrosion will also destroy the battery cables.

In addition to cleaning the terminals, a benefit of cleaner is that it will neutralize any acid on the outside of the battery.

Repair rating: Basic.

What you need: For this simple project, you should have a non-metallic stiff brush to rub off any build-up or corrosion, warm water mixed with dishwashing detergent, paper towels, steel wool or fine sandpaper, and a wrench to loosen the terminals.

What to do:
1. First remove the battery cables. If the battery has top terminals, loosen the nut on the side of the cable clamps. If it has side terminals, loosen the bolt in the center of the terminal. Always disconnect and remove the negative connection of the battery before working on the positive connection. Do not allow the negative connection to touch metal while the positive cable is still connected.

2. Clean both the terminals and the end of the cables with a non-metallic brush and a little warm water and dishwashing detergent. Be careful not to let the cleaning solution get inside the battery or run down to the tray under the battery, where it can cause corrosion. Wipe off the cleaner with paper towels, and dispose of them immediately and safely, so that the acid deposits do not contaminate or damage anything.

3. After cleaning, rinse the terminals and cable ends with clean water.

4. If the cables are corroded, clean them the same way.

5. With a bit of steel wool or fine grade sandpaper, shine the terminals and the inside of the cable connectors in order to ensure a good connection.

6. When cleaned, tightly reconnect the terminals. Replace and tighten the connectors in the reverse order of their removal.

7. To retard corrosion, apply a light coating of grease, petroleum jelly, or a protective spray specifically designed for that purpose.

Jump Starting a Battery

Most motorists have to "jump" start a car sometime during their driving career.

What can go wrong: A battery that is being drained without recharging will eventually run out of its stored electricity. This problem occurs if you leave the lights on for more than a few hours without your engine running, or if your electrical system is not properly recharging your battery. The car simply will no longer start. A jump start uses the energy from another car to get your engine going.

Repair rating: Basic.

What you need: To jump start a car with a dead battery, all you need is a set of jumper cables and another car that can start.

What to do:
1. Be sure that your jumper cable set is color coded (red for positive, black for negative) or that you can tell one cable from the other without fail! Cross-connecting, even for an instant, can damage both batteries, the charging system, and the ignition system, including the central control unit of the onboard computer, which is a very expensive part!

2. Connect the red cable to the positive (+) terminal of each battery. Again, be certain! They're usually marked, and the positive terminal is the larger of the two.

3. Connect one end of the black cable to the negative (-) terminal of the good battery.

4. Start the engine in the car giving the jump start.

5. Connect the other end of the black cable to the engine block or accessory clamp of the dead car, at least 12 inches from the dead battery.

6. Allow the good engine to run at least five minutes, longer if needed, to put a "surface" charge on the dead battery.

7. Start the dead engine.

8. Remove the jumper cables in reverse order; negative first, positive second.

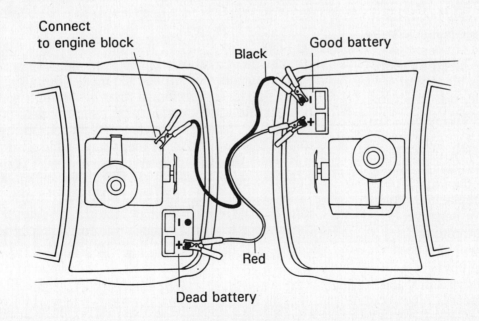

Connect to engine block

Black

Good battery

Red

Dead battery

The Jump Start

Replacing Battery Cable Clamps

A cable clamp is the device at the end of a battery cable that grips the terminal of a battery. Cable clamps are made mostly of lead, which resists corrosion from the sulfuric acid of the battery.

There are two basic types of cable clamps or terminals, top-mounted and side-mounted, which match the two different types of terminals on batteries. You can also replace the entire negative cable, but most problems result from broken or separated clamps.

Repair rating: Basic.

What can go wrong:
Neglect, mishap, or the passage of time can cause the corrosion, so that the clamps can't be cleaned or tightened properly. At this point, the clamps themselves must be replaced.

Tip: In the case of a short cable, such as the typical negative cable, it is easier to replace the entire cable.

What you need: When replacing a cable clamp, make sure you buy the same type that you are replacing. Polarity (positive or negative) is important on top-terminal types. You will also need strong cutting pliers or a hacksaw, a sharp knife, and some sandpaper.

What to do:
1. Remove the old clamp from the battery.

2. Cut the clamp off the cable, using the pliers or hacksaw. Cut as close to the old clamp as possible, leaving a maximum length of cable.

3. Use a sharp knife to slit the cable, and then carefully remove about a half-inch of insulation from the cable.

4. Use sandpaper or steel wool to clean the cable down to shiny copper.

5. Loosen the attaching bolts on the new cable clamp, slip it over the clean cable, and tighten. Repeat on the other cable, if necessary.

6. Reinstall the cables to the battery, positive first, negative last.

Battery Chargers

An alternative to jump starting a car is a battery charger. Battery chargers come in two basic types, current-controlled and voltage-controlled. The professional charger, or booster, is likely to be current-controlled and have high capacity: one hundred, two hundred, or two hundred fifty amps, adjustable in steps of a reasonable fifteen amps. Such a booster can put a quick surface charge on a battery in a few minutes. It can start a car with a dead battery, and it can charge several batteries at the same time.

Unfortunately, if left hooded up at too high a charging rate for too long a time, it can destroy a battery. Boosters usually come with timers to prevent such accidents. Battery chargers sold to do-it-yourselfers are usually of the voltage-controlled type. As a battery nears full charge, more voltage is required to push current through, so the voltage-controlled charger automatically cuts down the charging rate. They are often sold as "automatic" chargers. Sizes range from four amps up to forty or fifty amps.

Installing a New Battery

If you can't jump start your car, or you find that it won't hold a charge for more than a short period of time, you may need to replace it. A battery tester (see box on the following page) will indicate whether you should replace your battery. You can also have it checked at a service station.

To make sure that you are buying a fresh battery, shop at a store that does a high volume of battery sales. Such shops rotate their stocks, and any battery is likely to be fresh.

You can also buy a "Dry Charge" battery, which means that the electrolyte (a mixture of water and sulfuric acid) has not been put into the cells. If it is stored in a dry place, such a battery will remain fresh for many months. As soon as the fluid is added, the battery has about 75 to 80 percent of its fully charged power and can easily start an engine.

A better quality battery will last longer and will give better service along the way, so purchase one toward the top of the line. Batteries are generally rated by their expected life, which is based on length of warranty, cold cranking amps (CCA), and reserve minutes. Generally, the larger each number, the better the battery. A battery war-

ranted for five or six years is likely to cost more than a two-year battery; it is also guaranteed to last three times as long, and it likely will. A good quality battery is usually a better buy, especially if you intend to keep the car.

Extreme ranges of cold cranking amps are from 200 to 800 amps, but typical ranges are around 400 to 500 amps. Higher CCA allows a battery to crank a larger engine.

Reserve minutes are an estimate of the length of time that a battery can furnish electrical power to a car, after the alternator stops recharging the battery. Typical ratings are 60 to 80 minutes.

The longer the life, the more expensive the battery, but a good battery provides power and warranty coverage that are worth the investment.

Repair rating: Basic.

What you need: For tools you'll need your wrench and socket set, pliers, screw driver, petroleum jelly, and some sand paper or steel wool. You'll also need your new battery and probably a new clamp to hold it in place.

What to do: Batteries are heavy, so make sure you have a good grip when lifting it. Also, there's sulphuric acid

inside the battery, so wear old clothing. If any liquid from the battery gets on your skin, wash it off immediately with soap and water.

1. Disconnect both terminals of the old battery, disconnecting the negative connection first. Do not allow the negative connection to touch metal while the positive cable is connected.

2. The old battery must be disconnected from the clamps holding it in place. There are several different types of clamps, including top straps, top clamps, base clamps, and others. The clamping system will be obvious from inspection.

3. Once the battery is loose, carefully lift it out. Tip it up on one side to get your hand under, and remember that it's heavy.

4. After you remove your old battery, clean the tray that it sits on and inspect the device that holds the battery in place.

5. Clean the cable clamps with steel wool or fine sand paper, especially the inside. The shinier the better. If the old clamps are worn or corroded or if they won't clean up, replace them.

6. Place the new battery in the supporting tray, and secure it the same way in which the old one was secured. Make sure that it will not move around when you are finished.

7. When the new battery is in place, attach the positive terminal to the positive (+) cable and the negative (-) terminal to the negative cable. Double check these again, because a new battery will be ruined if it is hooked up backwards. Use wrenches, not pliers, to tighten the clamp bolts; then coat the terminals with a layer of petroleum jelly.

Battery Testers

There are several types of battery testers. One is a hygrometer, a glass or clear plastic tube with a bulb on one end and a "float" inside. This device measures the specific gravity of the electrolyte. Specific gravity can be converted to battery charge by referring to a chart, usually on the hygrometer. Hygrometers are very inexpensive and readily available.

Another type of tester is a "load" tester, which supplies a physical or electronic load to the battery and allows the observer to check battery performance under realistic conditions. Usually this type of equipment is available only to professionals.

You can also test a battery with a volt-ohm-milliammeter. This easy-to-use tool can be rented or purchased inexpensively and can help in a variety of repairs. In the DC volts position, one can read the voltage of the battery, normally about 12.6 volts or so. Then voltage can be checked while cranking to start the engine or with engine running. With engine running and alternator working, voltage will rise to 14 or 14.5 volts.

Battery Tip

Throughout this chapter we suggest disconnecting the negative terminal of the battery before doing electrical work. This will "open" the circuit and prevent electricity from flowing through the system. Once you disconnect the negative cable from the battery terminal, wrap it in some cloth to absolutely prevent any contact with metal or any scratches of your finish.

After your car's battery gets the engine started, its electrical supply is constantly replenished by the car's charging system.

Part of this system, the alternator, supplies the battery with electricity by changing mechanical energy (the rotation of the engine) into electrical energy. As its name suggests, the alternator, produces AC (alternating current), similar to household electrical current. It then converts this current to lower-voltage DC (direct current).

About 20 years ago, the alternator replaced the generator, which accomplished the same end. The advantages of the alternator are that it weighs less than a generator of similar output, and it is more efficient. It creates more electricity with substantially less drain on the engine.

The regulator is a device that senses the condition of the battery in the car. It adjusts the voltage and current output of the alternator so as to keep the battery fully charged while preventing damage from over-charging. Some regulators are built into the alternator case; others are separate devices mounted on the inside of the fender or on the firewall.

A basic owner's maintenance task is regular inspection of the drive belt that powers the alternator. Check this belt to the alternator for the correct tension. If it is too loose, your battery will not get the recharging it needs to stay healthy. If it is too tight, it may damage the alternator. Correct the tension if necessary, and the belt should be replaced if frayed or worn. More information on checking and changing the alternator belts, and an illustration of the belts system, is found in Chapter Four.

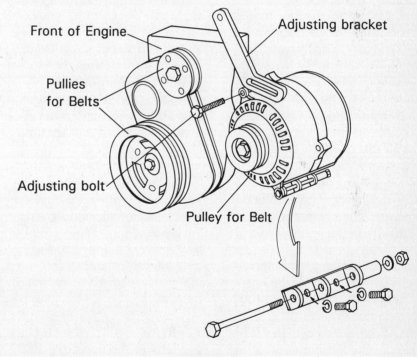

Front of Engine

Adjusting bracket

Pullies for Belts

Adjusting bolt

Pulley for Belt

Alternator

The alternator changes the mechanical energy of the engine into the electrical energy that operates the electrical system of the automobile. It also keeps the battery charged, by replenishing energy as it is used.

What can go wrong: An electrical connection within the alternator can fail, or a bearing can wear out.

Alternators are expensive, so make sure that's where the problem is before replacing it. Here's a reliable test: Jump start the engine, if necessary. With the engine running, disconnect the negative (-) terminal of the battery. If the engine continues to run, the alternator is working correctly. The regulator may be bad, the battery may be bad, there may be one or more corroded battery cable terminals, or there may be a wiring problem; however, the problem is not the alternator.

If a separate regulator is part of the system, it may become defective, so never assume the alternator is bad. If a new alternator is installed, the defective regulator can ruin it. Then, when a new regulator is installed, the now defective alternator may burn it out in fractions of a second. This can result in a very expensive series of "ping pong" failures. So always test first, or have a professional test the alternator for you.

Repair rating: Beyond Basic.

What you need: You'll need open or socket wrenches to loosen and re-tighten the mounting and adjusting bolts, a pry bar to re-tighten the drive belt, and a belt tension gauge.

What to do:
1. First, remove the negative battery terminal, and tie it securely in a shop rag. This will prevent damage to the new alternator and to the other electrical components of the car.

2. Remove all electrical connections to the defective alternator. These will vary from one make and model to the next. As you remove them, make a note, so you will know what goes where when you need to replace them.

3. Remove the defective alternator by completely removing all the holding bolts that keep it in position. Holding bolts, which can be mounting bolts or adjusting bolts, are in a variety of locations, depending on the make and model of the vehicle. Usually, there are two or three in number, and they will all be visible.

4. Install the replacement alternator, which must be physically and electrically identical to the original, in the same location as the original. Use the same nuts, bolts, washers, and mounting brackets.

5. Next, you'll need to tighten the belt, which we describe in Chapter Four.

6. Hook up the electrical connections, using the diagram you made earlier.

7. Start the engine, and test the alternator's output.

The ignition system is what starts your car and keeps it running. As its name Suggets, it ignites a mini-explosion in your pistons which provides power to your car. It consists of the battery, an ignition coil, a distributor, spark plugs, and different wires through which the electrical current passes.

The battery is constantly passing on the current it receives from the alternator to the ignition coil. The coil is a metal cylinder that converts the 12 volts DC (low voltage) from the battery into 12,000 volts AC (high voltage). This high voltage current passes through a wire to the distributor, which has wires connected to each one of the spark plugs. The distributor is called just that because it distributes the current sent by the coil to each of the spark plugs in their correct firing order.

The Underhood Decal is a label, usually found mounted on a fender wall, a valve cover, or elsewhere under the hood. It carries such information as model year, engine identification and displacement, air, fuel, and oil filter part numbers, spark plug type and recommended gap, recommended timing setting, diagram, diagram of the timing segment, and other useful information. Finding this decal will help you with many of your repairs, and especially while you are working with your ignition system. Location of the decal and specific information displayed vary greatly among different makes and models.

Replacing Your Distributor Cap

The distributor cap is the top part of your distributor. Typically, it contains an electrical contact point for each cylinder.

Note: Some high energy ignition caps, called "HEI", have the coil mounted internally, so they have no center wire.

What can go wrong: Age, heat, oil, and electrostatic damage can cause the distributor cap's terminals to corrode, or they can result in a crack or a high-voltage short circuit. The result is improper delivery of a high voltage spark to the spark plugs, which causes poor engine operation.

Repair rating: Basic

What you need: You'll need a new cap of the right type; ask at your parts store, because appearances can be deceiving. Anytime you replace a cap, you should replace the rotor as well, so you'll need a new rotor as well. The tip of the rotor and the electrodes in the cap form gaps of critical dimension. A plug boot puller will be helpful, and you may need a screwdriver, a nut driver, or needle-nose pliers, depending on how the cap is attached.

What to do:
1. With the wires still attached, remove the distributor cap from the body of the distributor. On HEI caps, a wiring connector must be removed before the cap is removed. Also on HEI caps, the coil must be removed from the old cap and installed in the new one.

2. Remove the old rotor. It may be simply pressed in position with a friction fit, or it may be attached with two screws.

3. Install the new rotor in exactly the same position as the old one.

4. Identify the locating tab on the new distributor cap. Install the new cap in exactly the same position as the old one, and be sure it is firmly mounted in place.

5. One at a time, move the wires from the old cap, and seat each one firmly in the same position in the new cap. Use the plug boot puller to remove each wire, with pressure from the bottom. Do not yank or twist the wires, which can damage them internally. Before installing each wire, check the end for corrosion. If present, remove it with fine sandpaper. If the corrosion cannot be removed, buy and install new plug wires.

6. Remove all tools, start the engine, and check for proper operation.

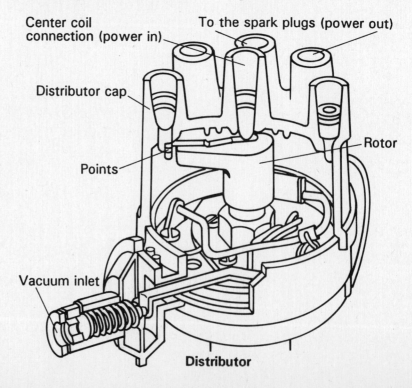

Center coil connection (power in)

To the spark plugs (power out)

Distributor cap

Rotor

Points

Vacuum inlet

Distributor

Spark Plugs

The spark plug delivers the high-voltage spark to ignite the fuel-air mixture in the combustion chamber of the cylinder of a gasoline engine.

A set of spark plugs can last from 10,000 miles on cars with conventional ignition systems to 18,000 miles on cars with electronic ignition. A new set of spark plugs once a year is a good investment to ensure fast winter starting, and it costs less than ten dollars in most cars. Your owner's manual will tell you exactly what type of plugs your car needs.

An important factor in the proper operation of your spark plugs is the distance between the two electrodes. This "gap" varies among engines. The proper gap distance can be found in your owner's manual, and it is measured by a special tool, a set of metal blades or wires, each of a different thickness.

An engine's firing order is based on the direction its distributor rotates and the order in which the cylinders are engineered to fire. Firing order varies from car to car, but cylinders are numbered from the front of the engine. A four cylinder engine most often has a firing order of 1-3-4-2, meaning that the number one cylinder fires first, then number three, number four, and number two. In V-8 engines there is no typical firing order. It is wise for a

do-it-yourselfer to change one spark plug wire or spark plug at a time to avoid disturbing the firing order. The problem is, if the engine were running badly because some wires were reversed, this method would perpetuate the error.

How to check them out:
Many mechanics use the spark plug as a simple diag-

nostic tool. The normal color for the spark end of the plug is light tan or gray. If you find the spark end is black, contains any goo, or appears to be damaged, you may need a complete tune-up, or you may have a problem that includes more than just the spark plugs (though such plugs will have to be replaced too).

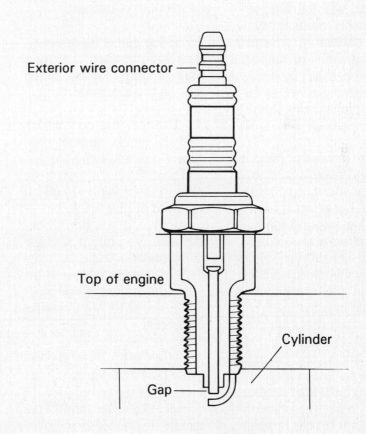

The Spark Plug

What can go wrong:

A spark plug is expected to wear out and be replaced. Spark plugs should last from 12,000 to 18,000 miles in normal conditions.

Repair rating: Basic

What you need: Most importantly, you'll need a set of the correct spark plugs for your engine. Your underhood decal will tell you, or your owner's manual may help. If necessary, your parts store has a chart for the spark plug number that you need. The numbering schemes for identical plugs differ from one plug manufacturer to another.

If your car needs "resistor" type plugs, make sure to buy them even if they cost more. There are hot plugs that extend farther into the combustion chamber, and cold plugs that are shorter. Do *not* arbitrarily switch to a hotter plug; you may cause severe internal damage.
The necessary tools are a swivel socket of the right size for your plugs; a drive extension, and a "Tee" handle or ratchet. You'll also need a few rags, a small soft brush (1 inch paint brush), a plug-boot puller, a plug "gapping" tool, and a small can or tube of anti-seize compound.

What to do:

1. With the correct plugs at hand, look up the gap for your engine. The gap is the distance between the plug's tip and its electrode. (Your underhood decal or owner's manual will tell you the proper distance.) Do not assume the new plugs are "pregapped" at the factory, which is impossible because the same plugs are used in different applications.

2. If the gap is incorrect, then you must set it, using a plug gapping tool and gentle taps on the electrode.

3. Use the plug boot puller to reach under the boot and gently pull and twist the boot and wire from the top of each plug. Never yank directly on the boot ot plug wire, because even if you don't break the wire, you might damage it internally.
   Note: Many do-it-yourselfers change one plug at a time, so as not to confuse the wires.

4. Use the brush to sweep away dust and debris in the vicinity of the plug. Use the socket, extension, and "Tee" handle or ratchet to remove the plug.

5. Apply a small dab of anti-seize compound to the threads of each plug, which is especially important when installing spark plugs in an aluminum block engine. Anti-seize compound helps prevent the steel plug from welding itself to the cylinder head by electrolysis, and it makes the next plug change easier.

6. Use your fingers to thread in the new plug as far as possible. Make sure it twists in smoothly. If it catches, you could be damaging the threads. When you're certain the plug is started correctly, cinch it down with the swivel socket, extension, and "Tee" handle. Do not over-tighten!

7. Replace the boot and plug wire. It requires a certain amount of "feel" to start the plug wire terminal onto the tip of the plug and a firm push to "seat" it. You may want to inspect inside the plug boot with a bright light, before replacing the wire.

8. Repeat the procedure for each spark plug.

9. The spark plug wires should be clean. Gently wipe them with a rag and don't yank on them. Clean off corrosion around the terminals of other wires and tighten the connections.

The Spark Plug Wires

Your car's secondary, or high voltage wires, usually referred to as spark plug wires, carry the high voltage from ignition coil to distributor, and from there to individual spark plugs. These wires have a fiber core saturated with carbon that conducts the spark, and they are covered by neoprene insulation and a tough outer covering.

What can go wrong: In the engine compartment, heat, oil, and acid attack the plug wires, and ozone, produced by the high voltage corona effect around the wires, can cause the wires to deteriorate. Older wires may be dull looking, hard, or brittle, and they may have a break in the internal conductor. These conditions can produce rough engine operation, hard starting, and poor gas mileage. Two or three years is a pretty good lifespan for a set of plug wires.

What you need: Be sure to buy the exact type of replacement wires for your car with factory installed terminals at each end. You'll also need a plug boot puller, spark plug wrench, pliers, and a rag.

What to do:
 1. To avoid disturbing your firing order, replace the wires one at a time, matching the length of each new wire to the old. Make sure the re- placement set is installed in exactly the same position as the old set. If the engine was firing properly, it should continue to work well.

2. Use the boot puller to remove the boot and wire from each plug. Trace it to its other end through the harness and retainer, and remove it from the distributor cap. A little force may be necessary. Don't hesitate to use pliers; you're replacing the wire, so you don't care if you break it.

3. Select a new wire of the same length as the one you removed. Install it, using the exact routing as the old wire. Push the terminals firmly into the cap and onto the plug.
 Note: A *tiny* bit of water as a lubricant will often make it easier to slip the boots into place on either end.

4. Repeat the process with each of the other plug wires, and finally with the coil-to-distributor wire.

5. Your new wires should be good for another two years.

 Owner alert: Some distributor caps use a screw to hold the wires in place. Usually the cap must be removed from the distributor to gain access to the set-screws.
 General Motors high energy ignition (HEI) distributor caps, and some others, have protective plates which hold down the plug wires and are clamped to the distributor cap. These clamps must be released, and the plates must be carefully removed, so as to not mix up the wires.

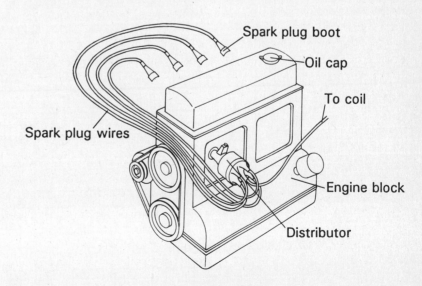

Spark Plug Wires

Your electrical accessories include the stereo, power antenna, heater, and air conditioner, electric door locks and fan, a trunk release, and the clock. Your fuse block is also an electrical accessory, although you may be less familiar with it.

Each of the electrical accessories in your car gets its power from the battery. An insulated wire carries electrical current from the positive terminal to every electrical element in the car. The wire from the negative terminal attaches to the car's metal frame in order to ground it.

To complete the electrical circuit, every electrical part of the car must either be bolted directly to ground, or must have a short grounding strap. Large metal assemblies, such as engine, body, and differential, are connected together electrically with heavy conductors also called grounding straps. A grounding strap can be very fine wire an inch or less in length or a cable as thick as your thumb and several feet long.

The fuses prevent too much current from flowing to the accessories. If one of your electrical devices fails, check the fuse box first!

Most of the components in your electrical system are too complicated to repair yourself except, of course, the lights. A few years ago a car owner equipped with a screwdriver could change any light on the car, including the headlights. That's still true for tail lights and overhead interior lights. But today's new aerodynamic designs are making some headlight changes out of the reach of the average driver.

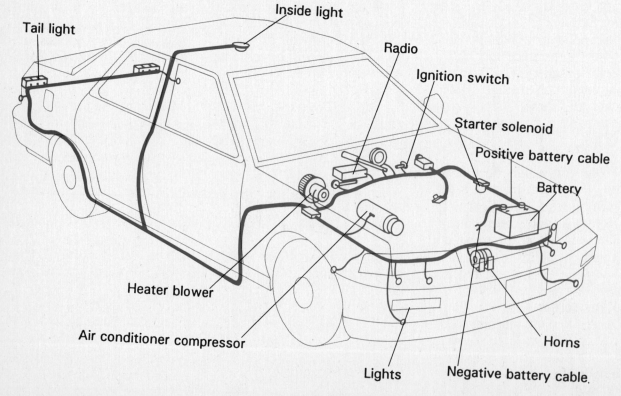

The Electrical System

The Fuse Box

The fuses protect the electrical items against a short circuit or an overload, and thus they prevent overheating, which could cause a fire or other expensive damage. When excessive current starts to flow, the fuse "blows out" by melting an internal resistor wire, to prevent further current from moving through this wire.

The fuse box is usually located under or near the dash, and in newer cars each fuse is labeled. Always check the fuse box first whenever anything electrical in the car fails to operate.

What can go wrong: In regular operation, a fuse can simply wear out. Otherwise, the blown fuse indicates a problem in an electrical device or in the wires serving it.

Repair Rating: Basic.

What you need: Carry a supply of spare fuses in your glove box, along with an inexpensive small fuse puller and installer. The fuse puller will help you remove the old fuse without breaking it or producing a shower of sparks. The fuses must be of the right type (check your owner's manual), and an assortment of different current ratings is desirable. Typical automotive fuses are 5, 10, 20, and 40 amps.

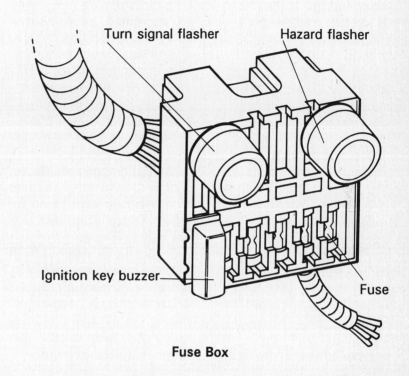

Fuse Box

What to do:
1. Locate your fuse box. These vary in appearance , but many are above and left of the brake or clutch pedal, beneath the dash and safely out of the way of your feet. Some are mounted on the "firewall," under the hood, usually on the driver's side.

2. Often, you can identify the blown fuse just by knowing which electrical device stopped working. The diagram in your owner's manual will also guide you.

3. Remove the blown fuse.

The two major types require different kinds of fuse pullers. Check the amps rating, and never install a fuse of larger current rating than specified, not even temporarily.

4. Install the replacement.

5. Turn on the device that had not been working. If it now works, you've solved the problem.

If it still does not work, and if you have replaced a proven bad fuse with a known good one, turn off the device and do not use it. You have a job better left to a mechanic.

Your Lights

Interior lights: If the overhead light in your car goes out, first check the switch. It may be in the off position. The switch usually has three positions: completely off, permanently on or a middle position which allows the light to go on whenever the car door is open. Look around the door frame near the hinges for a small button. This turns the light on and off. Push it a couple of times, as it may just be stuck. If the light does need to be replaced, simply remove the cover (most snap off), remove and replace the old bulb, and replace the cover.

Exterior lights: These lights are possibly the most important electrical accessories in your car. Not only do they allow the obvious benefit of night driving, but they are your main communication with other drivers.

You should occasionally check all your lights, which is a great deal easier with the help of another person. Have your helper turn on parking lights as you inspect both front and rear. Then check headlights on both high and low beams. Next test the brake lights, and then the turn signals at both front and rear. Your ignition must be on for these checks. If no turn signal lights come on, or if all four remain on without flashing, the cause is probably a defective flasher unit, located under your dash. Now test backup lights, again with ignition on. Keep track of any lights that need to be replaced.

If you notice brightening and dimming of headlights while driving at night, the problem may be anything from bad connections to a loose alternator belt, a bad regulator, or a defective alternator, among other things.

Start with a visual inspection. Look at battery terminal connections for cleanliness and tightness. Disconnect the negative terminal, and then check all connections to the regulator and alternator. Be sure all grounding straps are in place, clean, and tight. Check the condition and tension of the alternator drive belt. (For more information on how to check the belt, see Chapter Four.) Tightening or changing the belt may clear up the trouble. If none of these procedures resolve the problem, an auto electric specialty shop may be needed. Don't resort to guesswork. New alternators and regulators cost too much to resort to trouble shooting by substitution.

Tail Lights

Like the lights in your home, the light bulb in your tail light uses electricity to produce light. The lens, or plastic cover, protects the bulb and it also filters out all light except the desired color: red for the tail lights, red or amber for the turn-signal, white for backup, and amber for side lights.

What can go wrong: A bulb can burn out, or a lens can crack or break. This job is worth your time; replace any bulb by yourself and you'll save more than the price of the few tools you may need to buy.

Repair rating: Basic.

What you need: Tools and equipment needed vary from one model to another. On some models, bare hands are all you need, or Torx screwdrivers of the exact right size may be required.

What to do:
1. You must replace light bulbs or "lamps" with the correct replacements. Decide by the bulb number; appearances can be deceptive. Bring the old bulbs with you, to double check.

2. Lenses can be hard to find. For late model and popular cars, they're often stocked at dealers' parts counters. In other cases, they

can be ordered from a car dealer, which can take from a few days to two weeks. You can also check with an auto recycling yard, often called a wrecking yard.

3. Remove the old bulb. On some vehicles, you simply raise the trunk lid, twist the bulb housing 90 degrees counterclockwise, pull out the assembly, and remove the bad bulb. Other bulbs are re-

placed by pressing inward against spring tension, rotating counter-clockwise about 30 degrees, and removing the bulb.

4. Installation is the reverse of removal. Simply insert the new bulb and replace the assembly. Many bulbs have two locating "tangs," one shallower and one deeper. Before installing the new bulb, make sure it's lined up properly.

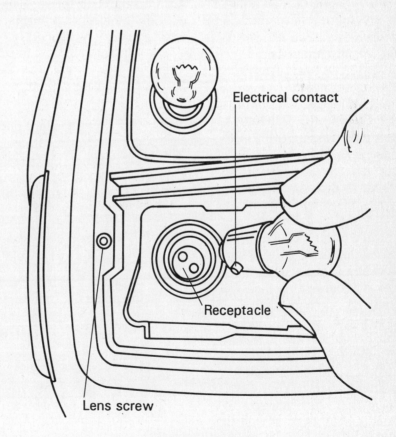

Tail Light Bulbs

91

Headlight Replacement

Obviously, the headlights are absolutely vital for night driving. Any problems should be taken care of immediately.

What can go wrong: The lights in your car, like the lights in your home, will burn out after a certain period of time. At that point, they must be replaced. However, getting at these lights is sometimes complicated, because the covers and other pieces involved are quite different from changing a light bulb in your home.

Repair rating: Basic.

What you need: You will need a replacement bulb from any parts store. In addition, you may need a Phillips or Torx screwdriver.

What to do: At the parts store, tell them the year, make and model of your car, and the exact location of each bulb you need. A headlight you buy for four or five dollars could easily cost $15 to $25 to have installed.

1. If your car has concealed headlights, turn the lights on in order to open the doors that hide them. Your owners manual will tell you how to keep the doors open with the lights off.

2. Remove the retaining screws on the headlight trim, and then remove the trim.

3. Remove the retaining screws to remove the retainer ring. If the ring has slots, loosen the three retaining screws, and turn the retainer ring counterclockwise until it can be removed. Be careful that the bulb does not fall out when you remove the retainer ring.

4. Pull the bulb forward and unhook the electrical wiring.

5. Attach the wiring to your new bulb, and replace it in the proper position.

6. Reattach the retainer ring and its screws.

7. Reattach the headlight trim and its screws, and reattach the headlight door if necessary.

8. Check the headlights on both low and high-beams. Headlights should be adjusted for the proper direction and illumination.

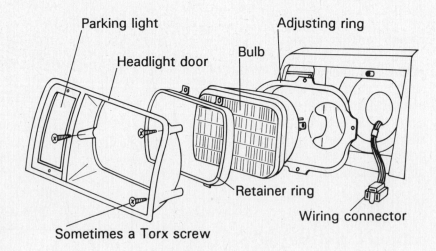

Parking light

Headlight door

Adjusting ring

Bulb

Retainer ring

Wiring connector

Sometimes a Torx screw

Replacing Headlights

The Fuel System

7

Your car's engine is called an internal combustion engine because its power is generated when an air and fuel mixture ignites inside the piston. The resulting explosion, called combustion, requires a spark, compression, and just the right mixture of fuel and air.

The fuel system delivers the air/fuel mixture to the engine. This system consists of a tank for storage, a pump to get the fuel to the engine, a fuel line from the tank to the air mixing system, and the air mixing system itself.

The most complex element in the fuel system is the air mixing device, which is either a carburetor or fuel injection system. In many cars today, fuel injection replaces the mechanical carburetor still found in many cars on the road. Repairs to these items must be left to the professionals.

This chapter will tell you how to keep the simpler elements of the system in top condition, and it will also discuss the most basic element, gasoline.

In This Chapter...
Your Carburetor or
   Fuel Injector
The Fuel Tank
The Fuel Line

The Fuel Filter
The Fuel Pump
The Right Gasoline

Your Carburetor or Fuel Injection System

Your car's engine mixes the proper proportions of air and fuel and then passes them to the cylinders. This proper ratio is fifteen parts air to one part fuel, by weight. An incorrect ratio will result in extra wear on the engine and lower mileage.

Air is drawn through an air cleaner or filter. It then passes to the mixing device: a carburetor or fuel injection system.

Carburetor: The carburetor is one of the most easily identified parts under the hood of your car. It is usually under the large, round housing for the air filter. To view the carburetor, remove the air cleaner housing by removing the wing nut found in the center of the lid and taking off the entire housing.

Fuel injection: Until recently, the main problem with fuel injection was that the mechanical controls were too slow to adequately operate at varying speeds and loads. Computer electronics changed all that. A microchip, with sensors that report everything from throttle position to exhaust composition, makes fuel injection systems more precise and quicker to respond

than a carburetor.

What can go wrong: Both systems fail to work properly when they deliver the wrong proportion of fuel and air. If your car stalls or accelerates improperly, the problem may be your carburetor or fuel injector.

What to do: Working with these systems is extremely difficult. There are at least 1300 current carburetor models, and over 200 fuel injection applications. Each is different, and proper care requires equipment and parts that are best left in the hands of a professional.

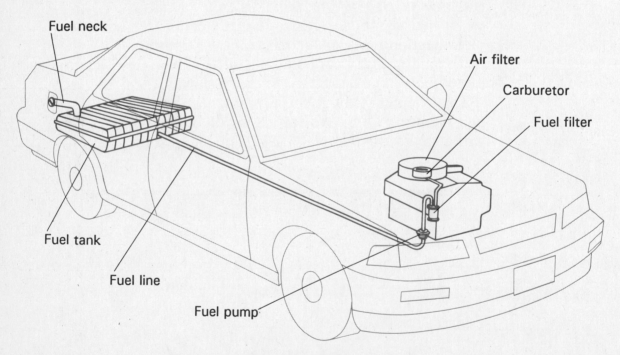

The Fuel System

The fuel system delivers the air/fuel mixture to the engine. It consists of a tank, a pump to get the fuel to the engine, a fuel line from the tank to the engine, and the air mixing system.

The Fuel Tank

Damaged, rusted, or leaking fuel tanks are usually replaced rather than repaired. Typical owner service means keeping them full and not allowing water and dirt to get inside.

The gas cap is actually an important part of your fuel system. If your gas cap is ever lost or stolen, replace it as soon as possible. The gas tank is part of a sealed system, and any opening leaves room for contamination. Rain, snow, leaves, twigs, or other debris can contaminate your fuel or clog the system.

Always keep in mind that any visible drip or strong odor of fuel is dangerous, and you should check it out (or have it checked) promptly.

What can go wrong: The empty space in your fuel tank is filled with air containing water vapor. In cooler weather, the water condenses on the top and sides of the tank, allowing water to mix with the fuel. The simple difference in temperature from day to night has the same effect. A drop of water today plus two drops tomorrow can add up quickly. Any rust formed by water vapor will settle at the bottom of the tank and cause problems if it builds up.

If water is drawn into the carburetor fuel bowl or injection system, the combination of fuel and water can cause damage to aluminum parts and can form a jelly-like deposit that settles and hardens like concrete.

Generally, however, this contamination does not cause harm, as the fuel filter works to prevent most clog ups. Nevertheless, consistently driving with only a small amount of fuel in your tank can choke up the system.

Exterior rust is also a problem. Sometimes a tank will rust simply because the manufacturer did not properly protect it from the elements. It can also start to rust if the protective coating has been scraped off. Fuel tanks can be expensive to replace, because the part itself is expensive. Call a wrecking yard to see if they have any tanks before settling on one from a car dealer.

What to do: Keeping your tank full will help, because there will be less air, and thus, less vapor, to cause problems.

To combat the problem another way, pour a can or bottle of anhydrous isopropyl alcohol into your tank twice a year. This fluid is marketed under dozens of brand names as a gas dryer or gas line antifreeze. The alcohol mixes with the water, and the mixture goes into your engine and burns off. A pint of alcohol will eliminate more than a pint of water.

Filling Your Tank

Be careful when filling your tank. The filler neck of the gas tank and the input tube of the car are connected by a flexible neoprene tube, clamped at both ends. In time, the neoprene deteriorates a bit, the clamps loosen a little, and a small amount of gasoline can leak. When filling up, insert the nozzle of the gas pump as far down the filler tube as it will go. When it kicks off the first time, stop filling. Sure, you can add another gallon or so, but that's the fuel that will leak.

The Fuel Lines

Engine fuel, either gasoline or diesel, is carried from the tank via one or more fuel lines to the engine. The illustration on page 94 will give you an idea of where the fuel line is located. Fuel lines are made of two materials, steel and a specially formulated neoprene hose. Neoprene fuel lines are sometimes covered with a woven steel armor for extra protection.

What can go wrong: Steel fuel lines rarely need to be replaced unless they have been involved in some kind of accident, or a stray rock from the road can kink or distort a line.

Neoprene fuel lines sometimes wear and fray because of heat, friction, or the passage of time. They must be replaced with similar lines. Never use a vacuum hose to replace a fuel line. It may look similar, but it is not stamped with the words "Fuel Line" along its body.

Repair rating: Adventuresome.

What you need: You'll need replacement line, a tubing wrench, and a plastic hammer or mallet. For a neoprene line, you also need pliers or a screwdriver to remove and replace the clamps holding the line in place.

If you need a new steel fuel line or a portion of one, order it from a dealer's parts department. Ordering it assures proper fabrication and good fit.

Fuel lines have very tight connections in order to prevent leaks. To loosen or re-tighten them, you need a tubing wrench. This tool slips over the tubing but grasps all surfaces of the fuel-line fitting. Using a regular wrench risks rounding the corners, which can make it impossible to remove the fitting without destroying it. Pliers or vise grips will also damage the fitting. A tubing wrench, once properly seated on the fitting, may be tapped with a plastic hammer or mallet to loosen a stubborn fitting. Finally, most of this will be done under the car, so a creeper and jack stands will be necessary.

What to do:
1. Raise and support the car with the jack stands.

2. Remove the damaged fuel line, using the tubing wrench. Have a container ready to collect fuel.

3. Position the new line in place and tighten the fittings. Steel fuel lines must be replaced with steel lines. Never substitute copper tubing, especially in an injection system. Copper does not tolerate vibration, fatigue, or pressure as well as steel.

4. To change a neoprene fuel line, simply remove the old line. Cut the new line to the correct length, using cutting nippers or a sharp knife. Install the new line, using the same clamps as were on the old line.

5. When the job is finished, start the engine and inspect carefully for leaks. Any fuel leak, no matter how tiny, must be stopped. Leaking gasoline can cause a fire or an explosion. Diesel fuel probably won't explode, but it can certainly burn. It's the same oil that's used in oil heating furnaces.

The Fuel Filter

In the hose between the fuel pump and the engine is a metal cylinder called the fuel filter. As fuel moves through this hose, the filter traps dirt, rust, sand, metal, and other abrasives that have mixed with the fuel. Replace the fuel filter every 10,000 to 12,000 miles, more often in severe conditions.

There are hundreds of models of fuel filters, and some vehicles have two or more. Diesel vehicles may have a water filter as well as a particle filter. Make sure you can get at the filter before buying one, as some are submerged in the fuel tank.

What can go wrong: By doing its job, the fuel filter becomes clogged with debris and contaminants. A reduced flow of fuel results in more air and less fuel than needed in the air/fuel mixture. Fuel economy and performance will suffer.

Repair rating: Basic for most, Beyond Basic for some integral filters, and Professional Only for submerged filters.

What you need: The tools vary, depending on your filter. You may need Corbin Clamp or ordinary pliers, screwdrivers, nut drivers (for screw-clamps), wrenches, or tubing wrenches. Use an old rag to catch fuel spill.

What to do:
1. Buy the exact replacement filter, and store it in its carton until ready for use. If short neoprene fuel hoses are included, clamp them onto the filter at this time.

2. Wipe the lines and area surrounding the old filter in order to prevent contamination while the line is open.

3. Remove the old filter and retain the connecting devices.

4. Install the new filter in the same position as the old one.

5. Tighten all fittings or clamps, but be careful not to overtighten, which can tear hoses and damage fittings, resulting in dangerous leaks.

6. Remove the towel, start the engine, and carefully check for any sign of a leak. A leak of any size must be corrected.

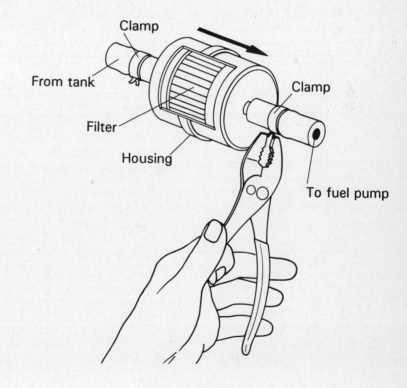

Clamp
From tank
Filter
Housing
Clamp
To fuel pump

Fuel Filter

The Fuel Pump

The fuel pump draws fuel from the tank, through the fuel line, to the carburetor or fuel injection system. There are many different kinds of fuel pumps, so check your owner's manual to find out what type you need. Our repair information applies to a typical *mechanical* pump.

Most electric fuel pumps are easier than this, but a few are more difficult. Submerged electric pumps, found in fuel tanks, are for professionals only.

Before replacing the pump, make sure that's really the problem. Problems which seem due to poor fuel supply may be caused by blocked fuel lines, a clogged filter, or a problematic carburetor.

If the fuel pump is the problem, buying a remanufactured replacement can save you half of the cost of a new one.

What can go wrong: The worst problem is a puncture on the neoprene diaphragm in a mechanical, engine-mounted pump. The engine may still run, but gasoline can slowly leak into the crankcase, where it mixes with the engine oil. If neglected, the gasoline will dilute the engine oil, reducing its lubricating ability. It can destroy the engine and can be a fire hazard. Any time your engine sounds louder than normal or you smell gasoline, check for this condition. The first indication is often that the oil level appears *higher* than the full mark.

Other pump problems include diminished pressure or volume, a blown fuse, a burned out electric pump motor, or an oil pressure interlock switch which is stuck open. Normally, this switch closes, to prevent engine damage if oil pressure is too low.

You can determine if roughness, stalling, or refusal to start is the fault of the fuel pump by a simple test.

1. Locate the hose that carries fuel from the fuel pump to the engine.

2. Unhook it at the engine end, and put the end of the hose into a clean can.

3. Have someone start the car while you watch for fuel to come out of the hose. If fuel comes out of the hose, the fuel pump is working, and the trouble must be somewhere up the line. Don't forget to turn off the engine before the gasoline overfills the can.

Caution: Be careful not to spill any gasoline, since it is highly flammable.

Repair rating: Beyond Basic.

What you need: The tools you need will vary from car to car. For a typical car manufactured in the mid-80's,

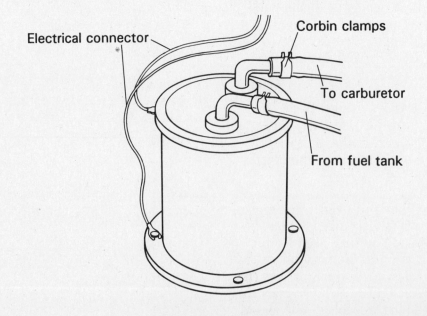

Electric Fuel Pump

you will need your wrench and socket set, a tubing wrench, pliers, gasket adhesive, and a pan or old towel to capture fuel spill.

Buy the exact replacement for the fuel pump. Many look alike, so take the old pump to the parts store, and describe the exact location on the engine block where it was mounted. The lever on the new pump must match the old one precisely.

What to do:
1. Place a pan beneath the fuel pump. Sometimes, if an air conditioner or other accessory blocks access to the fuel pump, you will have to work from beneath the car.

2. Remove the fuel lines from the pump. Depending on the model, this may require a tubing wrench or pliers to remove hose clamps. There are usually three hoses: one to the engine, one from the tank, and an overflow return hose to the tank.

Caution: When the line from the fuel tank is removed, be sure to clamp or plug it with a neoprene cork. Otherwise, the entire contents of the gas tank may drain out onto the ground!

3. Remove the two mounting bolts, one on each side of the fuel pump housing. These bolts and the holes through which they pass are

usually different sizes, which ensures that the new one cannot be installed incorrectly.

4. Remove the old pump. It may adhere to the engine, so tap it gently with a mallet to break the seal.

5. Carefully clean the mounting surface on the engine block. A scraper and gasket solvent may help. If the surface is not perfectly clean, an oil leak can occur.

6. Apply adhesive to both sides of the gasket. Stick the gasket onto the fuel pump, and place the two mounting bolts in position.

7. Place the new fuel pump in position. Check by feel that the lever of the new pump is centered on the lobe of the camshaft and not caught on one side.

8. Tighten the two mounting bolts, with fingers only at first, then with a socket or wrench. Check again that the lever is centered.

9. Replace and secure the fuel lines.

10. Start the engine and check for leaks. Any gasoline leak, no matter how small, must be corrected.

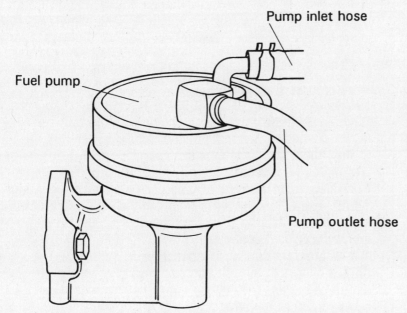

Pump inlet hose

Fuel pump

Pump outlet hose

Mechanical Fuel Pump

Choosing the Right Gasoline

Is there any real difference in the various brands of gasoline? Gasoline companies will tell you there is. However, most experts agree that most of the differences are not that significant.

Premium gasolines have a higher octane rating, more additives, and a higher price than regular gasolines. However, they do not burn cleaner, give your engine more power, or give your car better mileage than regular gasoline.

What does a gasoline's octane rating mean? The octane rating of a gasoline is not a measure of power or quality. It is simply a measure of the gasoline's resistance to engine knock. Engine knock is the "pinging" sound you hear when the air/fuel mixture in your engine ignites prematurely during acceleration.

The gasoline octane rating is on a yellow label on the fuel pump. Octane ratings vary with the different types of gas (premium or regular), in different parts of the country (higher altitudes require lower octane ratings), and between brands (Texaco's gasolines may have a different rating than Exxon's).

Most new cars are designed to run on a posted octane rating of 87. This number is the average derived from testing each gasoline under two different conditions, researched and measured.

Use this simple procedure to determine the right octane rating for your car:

1. Have your engine tuned to exact factory specifications by a competent mechanic, and make sure it is in good working condition.

2. When the gas in your tank is very low, fill up with the gasoline you usually use.

3. After you have driven 10 to 15 miles, come to a complete stop and accelerate rapidly. If your engine knocks (that pinging sound) during acceleration, switch to a higher octane rating.

4. If there is no knocking sound, wait until your tank is very low, and then fill up with a lower rated gasoline. Repeat the test. When you reach the level of octane that causes your engine to knock during the test, go back to the next highest rating.

Note: Your engine may knock when you are accelerating a heavily loaded car up a hill or when the humidity is low. This is normal and generally does not mean you need a higher octane gas.

Using Oxyfuels

More than ever, gasoline has a bewildering array of components touted as octane boosters or pollution fighters. Some urban areas with carbon monoxide pollution problems require the use of oxygen-containing components (called oxyfuels), such as ethanol and MTBE (methyl-tertiary-butyl-ether).

The use of these compounds is not without controversy. Some car companies recommend their use; others caution against them. Most companies approve the use of gasoline with up to 10 percent ethanol, and all approve the use of MTBE up to 15 percent. Many car companies recommend against using gasoline with methanol, alleging that it will cause poorer driveability, deterioration of fuel system parts, and reduced fuel economy.

Manufacturers that warn against using methanol or other additives may not cover the cost of warranty repairs if these additives are used, so check your owner's manual and warranty to determine what additives are covered. Also check the gas pump, as many states now require the pump to display the percentage of methanol and ethanol in the gasoline.

Avoid Gas Saving Devices

So-called gas saving devices should be avoided. There are literally hundreds of products on the market that claim to save you money at the gas pump. Not only do the majority of them fail to work, but some may even add to your repair costs.

Many of these gadgets feed extra air into your PCV line, claiming that your engine will "breathe better." By introducing too much air, they cause an engine to run lean. But you can't fool your fuel system. Running either richer or poorer than the correct air to fuel ratio actually causes your mileage to drop off.

Keep in mind that no matter what the promotional materials say, no government agency endorses any of these products. In fact, the Environmental Protection Agency (EPA) tests many of the products, and, of over 100 products tested, only six actually improve fuel efficiency. Even these six products offer only limited savings because of their cost and relatively small improvement in fuel efficiency.

None of these products are readily available, but the one that seems most common is a device that automatically turns off your air conditioner during periods of rapid acceleration. It reduces engine drain and may increase fuel economy by 4 percent. How-ever, it only works when you are using your air conditioner. It is marketed under the names Pass Master Vehicle Air Conditioner Cutoff and P.A.S.S Kit.

Warning: If your car has a catalytic converter, do not try to alter it or take it out. It is against the law, and you could damage your engine or invalidate your warranty.

If you are interested in more information on products that claim to save gas, write to the National Technical Information Service, Springfield, VA 22162.

Caution!

o *Never* carry gasoline in a can anywhere in your car. Carry your fuel reserve in the bottom half of your gas tank, and drive off the top half.

o *Never* use gasoline as a solvent to clean dirty parts. In addition to the fire hazard, gasoline contains lead and other poisons which can enter your body through your skin. Standard solvent and kerosene are a great deal safer, and they're cheap and widely available.

o *Never* pour gasoline into your engine in an attempt to start a balky engine. Liquid gasoline, when poured into an engine that may be malfunctioning already, can produce a spectacular explosion and a fire. Instead, purchase a pressure spray can of starting fluid. It will start your car more readily and safely than gasoline, even in very cold weather, and the spray makes quantities easy to control.

Products That Don't Work

Purported gas-saving devices come in many forms. Listed below are the types of products on the market. Under each category are the names of devices actually reviewed or tested by the EPA, for which there was *no evidence of any improvement in fuel economy.*

AIR BLEED DEVICES
ADAKS Vacuum Breaker Air Bleed
Air-Jet Air Bleed
Aquablast Wyman Valve Air Bleed
Auto Miser
Ball-Matic Air Bleed
Berg Air Bleed
Brisko PVC
Cyclone - Z
Econo Needle Air Bleed
Econo-Jet Air Bleed Idle Screws
Fuel Max
Gas Saving Device
Grancor Air Computer
Hot Tip
Landrum Mini-Carb
Landrum Retrofit Air Bleed
Mini Turbocharger Air Bleed*
Monocar HC Control Air Bleed
Peterman Air Bleed*
Pollution Master Air Bleed
Ram-Jet
Turbo-Dyne G.R. Valve

DRIVING HABIT MODIFIERS
Fuel Conservation Device
Gastell

FUEL LINE DEVICES
Fuel Xpander
Gas Miser I
Greer Fuel Preheater
Jacona Fuel System
Malpassi Filter King
Moleculetor
Optimizer
PETRO-MIZER
POLARION-X
Russell Fuelmiser
Super-Mag Fuel Extender
Wickliff Polarizer

FUELS AND FUEL ADDITIVES
Bycosin*
EI-5 Fuel Additive*
Johnson Fuel Additive*
NRG #1 Fuel Additive
QEI 400 Fuel Additive*
Rolfite Upgrade Fuel Additive
Sta-Power Fuel Additive
Stargas Fuel Additive
SYNeRGy-1
Technol G Fuel Additive
ULX-15/ULX-15D
Vareb 10 Fuel Additive*
XRG #1 Fuel Additive

IGNITION DEVICES
Autosaver
Baur Condenser*
BIAP Electronic Ignition Unit
Fuel Economizer
Magna Flash Ignition Ctrl. Sys.
Paser Magnum/Paser 500/Paser 500 HEI
Special Formula Ignition Advance Springs*

INTERNAL ENGINE MODIFICATIONS
ACDS Auto. Cyl. Deactivation Sys.
Dresser Economizer*
MSU Cylinder Deactivation*

LIQUID INJECTION
Goodman Engine Sys. Model 1800*
Waag-Injection System*

MIXTURE ENHANCERS
Basko Enginecoat
Dresser Economizer
Electro-Dyne Superchoke*
Energy Gas Saver*

Environmental Fuel Saver*
Filtron Urethane Foam Filter*
Gas Saving and Emission Control Improvement Device
Glynn-50*
Hydro-Catalyst Pre-Combustion System
Lampkin Fuel Metering Device
Petromizer System
Sav-A-Mile
Smith Power and Deceleration Governor
Spritzer*
Turbo-Carb
Turbocarb

OILS AND OIL ADDITIVES
Analube Synthetic Lubricant
Tephguard*

VAPOR BLEED DEVICES
Atomized Vapor Injector
Econo-Mist Vacuum Vapor Injection System
Frantz Vapor Injection System*
Hydro-Vac
Mark II Vapor Injection System*
Platinum Gasaver
POWER FUEL
SCATPAC Vacuum Vapor Induction System
Turbo Vapor Injection System*
V-70 Vapor Injector

MISCELLANEOUS
BRAKE-EZ*
Dynamix
Fuel Maximiser
Gyroscopic Wheel Cover
Kat's Engine Heater
Lee Exhaust and Fuel Gasification EGR*
Mesco Moisture Extraction System
P.S.C.U. 01 Device
Treis Emulsifier

* For copies of reports on these products, write Technical Evaluation Branch, EPA, 2565 Plymouth Road, Ann Arbor, MI 48105. For reports on the other products, contact the National Technical Information Service, Springfield, VA 22162. (703-487-4650).

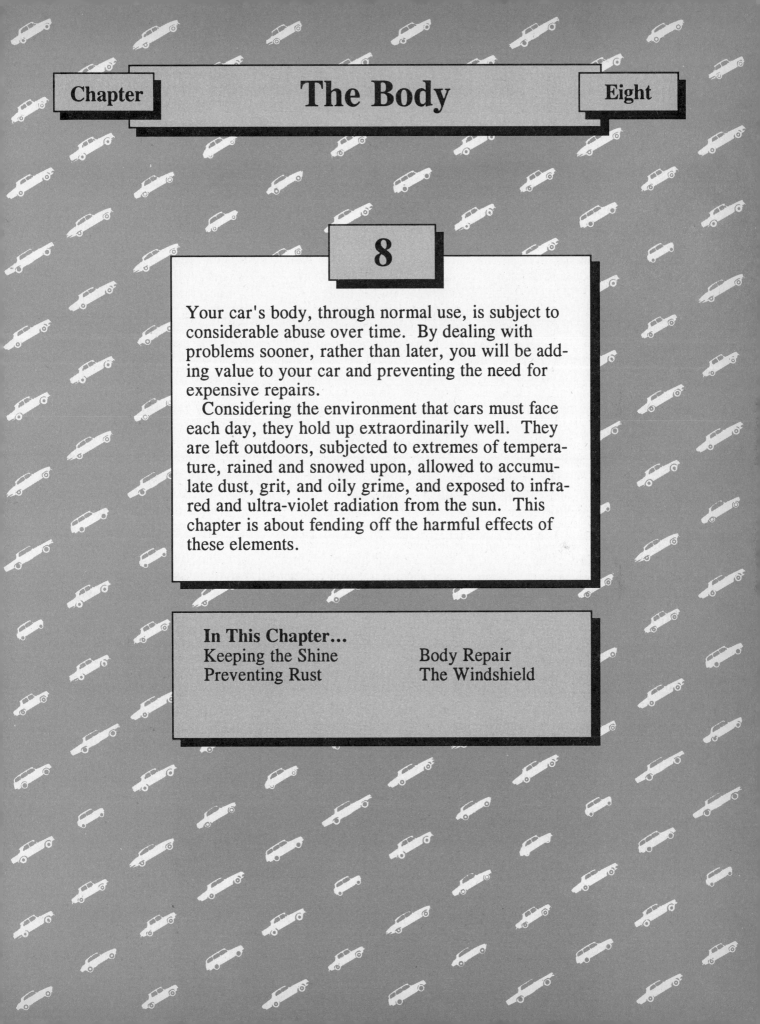

8

Your car's body, through normal use, is subject to considerable abuse over time. By dealing with problems sooner, rather than later, you will be adding value to your car and preventing the need for expensive repairs.

Considering the environment that cars must face each day, they hold up extraordinarily well. They are left outdoors, subjected to extremes of temperature, rained and snowed upon, allowed to accumulate dust, grit, and oily grime, and exposed to infrared and ultra-violet radiation from the sun. This chapter is about fending off the harmful effects of these elements.

In This Chapter...

Keeping The Shine

Keeping your car clean and shiny is important not only for its appearance but also to preserve the finish. While you can clean the inside of your car at irregular intervals, regular exterior cleaning is a must for making the finish last.

Washing and waxing your car will protect the surface of the paint from harmful elements in the environment, such as water vapor, ozone, and ultra-violet radiation. Other factors, such as dust, acid rain, and salt can open up tiny cracks in the surface of the finish. If these elements are not washed away, your car may begin to rust. Since few factors affect the value and life of your car as much as the condition of its body, regular cleaning and waxing are imperative.

Today's paint and finish jobs are better than ever before. With proper care, you can easily expect your car's paint job to last for years. The key to long life is to treat the finish carefully. Because of the protective finish that comes on a new car, regular washing will be sufficient for the first two years of the car's life. After the two year mark, begin a regular waxing routine.

Washing: Commercial car washes may seem like a convenient alternative to doing it yourself, but be careful, because some can harm your car's finish. If the car wash uses too little water or doesn't properly filter recycled water, your car may remain dirty and can even be scratched. Avoid car washes that use plastic strip brushes; cloth pads are better for your car. The best are "frictionless" washes, which use high pressure water and special detergents and don't use brushes or pads.

Hand washing your car is preferable to automatic car washes. Here are some simple pointers that will help you to get the best shine and avoid scratches.

Always work in the shade; excessive heat may stain wet paint. Rinse the car with water from a hose rather than a bucket. Never wipe a dry car with a dry cloth, because tiny particles of dirt can scratch the paint.

To wash your car, use either a very soft cloth or the big, floppy mittens sold specifically for this purpose. Gentle household cleansers, such as mild dishwashing liquid, are safe and economical. You don't have to purchase "special" car washing detergents. Avoid spray household cleaners and laundry detergents which may damage, discolor, or leave a film on the paint.

Starting at the top and working your way down, hose off the car, clean one area with warm, soapy water, and rinse it off. By hosing off each section as you wash it, you prevent the suds from drying on the car.

Loosen hard-to-remove dirt by placing a wet rag on it for a few minutes, rather than trying to scratch it off. There are commercial products available to clean off dead bugs and other stubborn spots. Always spray the car's wheel wells and underside to loosen debris.

When the job's completed, towel dry the car, and make sure that no water remains in the rust-prone areas around the trim and bumpers.

You can clean the mirrors and windows with the same products that you use in your home. The windshield wipers lift away from the car so that you can clean under them. Clean the wipers as well, to prevent a dirty wiper from scratching the glass.

Use mild soap or dish detergent to clean dirt and grease off tires. A scrub brush or scouring pad will remove stubborn stains, but be sure to wet the tires first. Never use gasoline or kerosene to clean tires. If your white walls are extremely dirty, use a special whitewall cleaner or a steel wool scouring pad. Extremely scuffed tires can be painted with "tire black," available at auto supply stores.

104

Waxing

Although professional waxing is costly and doing it yourself requires time and effort, the benefits of a good wax job are numerous.

Once your car is two years old, plan to wax it once a year, although twice a year is preferable. Waxing seals the car's finish. You can easily tell that your car is due for a waxing when water droplets don't bead up on its surface.

If you use an automatic car wash, don't waste your money on hot wax sprays. They offer little protection.

Two step process: After thoroughly washing your car, deep clean the old finish with a cleaner/polisher. This product contains a very mild abrasive, which cleans off the oxidation and fills in the little scratches. Then, after using the cleaner/polisher on your car, it's ready to wax. Because the cleaner/polisher leaves the surface exposed to the elements, the wax is necessary to seal in the beauty of your hard work.

While the two-step waxing process is the best way to protect your car's finish, there are also one-step car waxes on the market. These will not provide as deep a shine, but they are perfectly adequate.

There are a variety of waxes to choose from, including liquid, soft, and hard. The liquid waxes are easiest to apply and are suitable for touch ups, but they don't last nearly as long as the other types. Soft waxes are easy to apply and remove, and many contain safe, light cleaners. Hard waxes provide more protection and they last longer than liquid or soft waxes. Apply these to one small area at a time to prevent the wax from hardening too much.

Try to avoid cleaners and waxes that contain abrasives, or use them only occasionally. Always follow the directions, using soft rags to apply the wax, remove it, and rub the car until it shines.

Poly-sealant products, which contain polymer substances and can be found in auto supply stores, are reputed to be more effective and longer lasting than wax. New car dealers sometimes try to sell these same substances to customers for hundreds of dollars. Read the directions before you buy, because the process is time consuming. (You have to wash and polish your car before you apply the polymer.) If you wax often, you really don't need a sealer. These products claim to retard the spread of rust, but there's not much evidence to prove it.

Professional Polishing Instead of Repainting

If your car's finish is dull, before you repaint, consider a professional polish job. Repainting a car is very expensive, and, unless it is done with a tremendous amount of precision and care, it won't be as good as the original job. Only repaint if your car looks dull and lifeless and the streaks in the paint don't come out even when you wax.

A professional polishing job involves rubbing away the top layer of paint with various rubbing compounds and cleaners. Once this is done, the nicks are touched up, and the whole surface is covered with one or more coats of top-grade wax. A good professional's skill is not in the waxing but in rubbing away just enough paint without destroying the color. You can often find a professional working out of a car wash or gas station. While the price may sound expensive, compare it to the cost of a paint job.

Tip: If your car absolutely needs a paint job, sticking to the original color will save you money and look better than a color change. Changing colors requires extra work on the fenders, trunk and doors, which can be costly.

Preventing Rust

Not only is rust one of the most insidious hazards to your car, but a rust problem will depreciate the value of your car more than any other automobile repair problem. A bad engine can usually be replaced more easily and less expensively than major body parts ruined by rust and corrosion. Your best protections against the ravages of rust and corrosion are regular cleaning and periodic inspection.

Early rust is recognized by a light brown stain. Don't ignore it. Heading off trouble early will save money in the long run. But if you miss the early rust signs and the problem continues, buying a new car is not the only solution. Major rust problems can be repaired. If you find rust on a chrome part, however, complete replacement with a recycled part is the most economical solution.

A major cause of car rust in the United States is the millions of tons of road salt used to treat winter roads. Salt works its way upward, carried by moisture, into every nook and cranny of the car. In fact, salt causes car rust in spring more often than in winter. The reason is rising temperatures, which induce salt-caused oxidation. Likewise, leaving your car in a heated garage in winter can also speed up salt corrosion. Acid rain, another factor, at-

tacks paint and removes the metal's protective barrier.

With all the fear associated with the potential rusting of your car, many car owners wonder whether they should get their car rustproofed. The answer: No. In fact, today's new cars come with very good built-in corrosion protection and very good warranties against corrosion. In addition, the very act of rustproofing a car after you have driven it for a while may do more to cause rust than to prevent it. You may be sealing in the corrosive materials that you are trying to protect against. In addition, most rustproofing programs involve drilling holes into various parts of the car to spray material inside those parts. Drilling these holes breaks the manufacturer's seal against corrosion, and, ironically, it is in these holes that rust usually starts. In fact, some manufacturers, such as Toyota, specifically recommend against rustproofing.

There are other problems with rustproofing, as well. You are probably paying for coverage overlapping your warranty, rustproofing often requires expensive inspections, and some consumers have paid for rustproofing only to find that nothing was even sprayed inside. In short, rustproofing is expensive and of negligible value.

And if that's not enough, many car makers caution that rustproofing may void your corrosion warranty.

A far better course of prevention is to keep the exterior and undercarriage of your car clean and to have a good understanding of what's covered under your new car corrosion warranty.

A word about undercoating: Undercoating is not rustproofing; it is a sound-deadener. If any moisture, salt or other material is trapped beneath it, or if it later cracks, undercoating can actually accelerate the rusting process.

How to really prevent rust:

O Keep your car clean, wash it frequently, and wax it as often as possible.

O Hose down the underside every two months and more often if you live in an area where salt is used.

O Take care to rinse out the wheel wells and clean out leaves or other debris that retain moisture.

O Keep the drain holes in the frame, floors, and bottoms of the doors free.

O Leave your doors open for a few minutes to let all the water drain out after you wash your car.

Paint Touch-Ups

Scratches and nicks in the finish of your car provide an open pathway for water and ultraviolet rays to attack the metal of your body. In a surprisingly short period of time, rust and corrosion "creep" along the sheet metal beneath the surface of good paint, resulting in expensive damage.

Owner service is easy. You can buy small bottles of paint that match your finish perfectly. These look similar to nail polish bottles, and they have a brush mounted in the cap. Your new car dealer should have them in stock if your car is a fairly current model. Professional automotive paint supply stores offer a larger selection, and they will sell you individual bottles.

The dealer or paint store will need the number or letter code for the exact paint on your car. Location and coding vary from one model to the next, but both the dealer and the paint store have charts and can tell you where to look; sometimes they'll even look themselves.

What to do: Clean the area you're going to touch up with a grease-cutting cleaner. Do *not* use acetone or paint thinner; they may melt the old finish. Shake the bottle thoroughly, wipe most of the paint off the brush, and apply the paint to the bad spot. If you need two coats, be patient and observe the drying time printed on the label. Waxing the area after the paint has thoroughly dried will help it blend in.

When you're finished, be satisfied that you have protected your car against future rust damage.

Lubricating Door Hinges

What can go wrong: Lack of lubrication can make the hinges squeak. More than a mere annoyance, if neglected, these squeaks can lead to premature wear and costly hinge failure.

Repair rating: Basic.

What you need: All you'll need is a can of spray lubricant, such as WD-40 or LPS-1, and a shop rag.

What to do: Open the car door. Move it back and forth to observe and identify the hinges and other moving parts. Attach the plastic spray hose to the tip of the can of lubricant. Direct a short burst of spray at each hinge; there will be two per door. Move the door back and forth to allow the lubricant to work in, wipe up any excess with the shop rag. Don't forget your hood and trunk hinges!

Car Tops and Covers

Beware of Car Covers: If you often park your car outside, you may have bought a car cover to protect it. But a car cover will not protect your car from moisture. In fact, vinyl or waterproof car covers actually trap moisture under the cover and prevent it from evaporating. A car with a waterproof cover will retain moisture all day, while one without a cover will dry in the sun after a rain.

Car covers are often more trouble than they are worth. But if you decide you do want one, make sure it is 100 percent cotton, so it will dry out quickly and allow moisture to evaporate easily. It should also be tightly woven in order to keep out the sunlight. Avoid car covers with metal grommets that can scratch your finish.

Convertible Tops: If you have a convertible top, keep it clean by vacuuming it or sweeping it with a whisk broom. The metal mechanism should be clean and oiled so that the top maneuvers smoothly. A coat of wax on the metal parts will help prevent rusting. Make sure that the well into which the top folds is also kept clean and free of debris.

If your convertible has a plastic rear window, the window may become cloudy from oxidation. Check in the auto section of a department or parts store for a conditioner that can remove some of the cloudiness. Since the sun oxidizes the window and makes it cloudy, try not to park with the plastic window in direct sunlight for long periods of time.

Vinyl Tops and Trim: The best thing you can do to make your vinyl top last is to wash it regularly. Never wax it. The abrasives in the wax can damage the thin coating of clear acrylic that protects the top and gives it its shine. To wash a vinyl top, use a mild soap, lukewarm water, and a soft bristle brush. Regularly remove residue so that it won't be ground into the vinyl.

After two or three years, you may notice dullness or fading in the top. If so, follow the regular cleaning with a vinyl top dressing, available in most parts stores. Consistent application, about four times a year, will protect and extend the life of a new vinyl top.

If your vinyl top rips, cover the tear with tape until you can have it repaired. There are vinyl repair kits available to do the job. Choose a simple kit and follow the instructions carefully. If your vinyl roof is beyond repair, an auto upholstery shop can replace the vinyl with material.

Keep a sharp eye out for tiny bulges or bubbles in the top. They may indicate rust pockets forming under the vinyl. This rusting is one of the hazards of a vinyl roof, and repair can be very expensive. If you find any bubbles, press on them gently. If they seem hard and crunchy, rust may already have started. If they feel like air bubbles, carefully pierce them with a sharp object and try to squeeze the air out. If some adhesive comes out, wipe it off quickly and your problem should be solved. If nothing comes out or the bubble pops up again, use a glue injector and fill the bubble with glue. Then carefully squeeze out the excess until the vinyl lays flat.

Body Repair

Earlier cars were built on a heavy, steel frame, or chassis, which provided the car's underlying strength. Body components were bolted to the frame and could be replaced one at a time without affecting the strength or integrity of the car.

Today, most cars are built with a unitized body. With a unitized body, an entire cage is built, onto which various parts of the car are attached. This cage is a complete unit, thus the term "unitized" body.

Eliminating the heavy, awkward frame makes the car much lighter, and it improves mileage. The disadvantage is that after a collision, certain body parts and panels cannot simply be unbolted and replaced with new ones. Nor can they be "hammered out" and painted, as was formerly possible. Special equipment and techniques are needed for a body shop to restore the body to within millimeters of original dimensions and to make sure that the original strength is restored.

If you need body work because of a major rust problem or accident, get it done as soon as possible. You will prevent the damage from getting any worse and avoid risking the structural integrity of your car.

The tools and expertise required for fixing dents and deep scratches are considerable, so most body repair is best left to the experts. However, constantly going to the body shop with every little dent adds considerably to your operating expenses. Consider waiting to have all your minor repairs done at the same time. The cost will be far less, and you will reduce the time your car is out of service.

Between repair shop visits, take care of any exposed metal. Regular waxing will help, and you should buy a small can of paint from your car dealer for minor touch ups. Most car dealers will have the exact color, you need often it comes in a little container with a brush built into the cap.

When shopping for body work, a common practice is to get three estimates. This technique does not mean that you should necessarily choose the cheapest. Investigate shops recommended by friends and always get a written estimate.

While you are waiting for the estimate, look around at the cars being worked on. Looking at a body work job before the final painting can tell you a lot about how well it was done. Get close to the car and squint down along the area being worked on. Look for ripples, rough places, or bulges. When looking at finished work, resist the temptation to check the job by running your hand over the smooth paint. It may feel like silk but look horrible in the daylight. It's how it looks, not feels, that's important.

Make sure that all the items on the estimate are written clearly and that you understand them. Will you be getting new or used parts? Used parts are fine, but make sure you're not paying new part prices. Not only are used parts cheaper than new parts, they may actually fit better than a new part. See the following box on certified parts.

If many parts are involved and you have the time, consider finding the parts yourself at a local wrecking yard. Many body shops will be happy to let you supply the parts, as long as you can find the right ones.

There are several other ways to save. Contact local high schools, technical schools, or body shop schools. The work, if the teacher is a professional, will often be first rate. If you need to replace some chrome trim and can't find an exact match, check with a body shop to see how much they would charge to remove the rest of it and fill the little holes that used to attach it. If you have an older car, you may be surprised to find that this job is a lot less expensive than paying for hard to find replacement parts. You can also have the estimate divided into parts according to the type of work to be done: reassembly, body work, and painting. You may find less expensive painting at an otherwise more expensive shop, so it pays to have one shop do the body work and another to paint the car. Finally, make sure to find out when the car will be ready and what type of guarantee the shop will offer to cover the work done.

Certified Automotive Parts

A few years ago, in order to save money on car repairs, many insurance companies began to consider the use of body parts made by companies other than the car manufacturers. Because there had been little competition, the car companies had charged exorbitant prices for these parts. It was quite common to find a car company fender costing $250 and its generic equivalent at around $50.

There were, however, questions about the quality of the generic parts being substituted. In order to ensure that the quality of these parts was standardized, the insurance industry set up a non-profit certification organization to develop and implement manufacturing and quality standards for crash repair parts. This organization is similar in concept to Underwriters Laboratory, which was also started by the insurance industry.

Today, the Certified Automotive Parts Association, called CAPA, certifies the quality of a number of crash repair parts. Because not all body parts meet these standards, it's important to insist on CAPA certified parts. Each part that meets the standards has a CAPA seal with a unique number. If the part doesn't have a seal, then it is not certified.

Parts that have been certified include fenders, hoods, bumper covers, door panels, and grilles. If the part is certified, then it meets rigorous, fit, material, corrosion resistance, and quality standards.

Warning: Clipped Cars

A "clipped" car is one that has been reconstructed from the parts of two or more cars. If a car has been severely damaged in the rear and an identical model has been damaged in the front, it is not uncommon for the two cars to be cut in half and the good front attached to the good rear.

Unibody cars that have been welded in this manner can be dangerous. These cars simply do not hold up in accidents, because the welding process required to connect the parts is extremely difficult. If welding is not done properly, the strength of the unibody shell will be severely diminished. Vehicle Support Systems of Scottsdale, Arizona crash tested and investigated some of these cars to observe the occupant protection they offered. In an actual crash test, the clipped car literally split in half along the welds.

Replacing parts on a steel frame car does not generally diminish protection. As long as the steel frame is intact, it is relatively easy to add body parts without compromising safety.

Towing a Car

We generally do not recommend towing a car with another car. You may do serious damage to both cars.

However, if you must tow a car yourself, never use a metal chain. A chain is too inflexible, and it is extremely hard on the transmission of the towing car and the bumper of the car being towed. Also, use cotton or nylon rope only as a last resort; it is often too flexible or not strong enough to hold a car securely. Its flexibility could also cause a dangerous oscillating action.

For a do-it-yourself tow, the best aid is a nylon tow strap, which you can find at any parts store. A strong hook on each end hooks back over the strap. The strap is two to three inches wide and about an eighth of an inch thick, with enough flexibility to avoid jerking and enough firmness to avoid oscillation.

Before you start towing, work out a set of hand signals with the driver of the car being towed. The driver of the towing vehicle must be in complete charge and must signal all starts, stops, and turns to the other driver.

The Windshield

The Windshield Washer:
One of the most useful features of your car is the windshield washing system, which sprays your windshield with cleaner at the touch of a button.

What can go wrong:
Having an empty reservoir can be a safety hazard if you are on the highway and your car gets sprayed with mud or salty water. Often, just as the rain starts, your windshield wipers streak and you have a need for cleaner. You should always keep the reservoir full.

What to do: The windshield washer reservoir is a transparent plastic bottle located in the engine compartment. Sometimes it is located near the coolant recovery tank. They are similar in appearance, so don't confuse the washer reservoir with the coolant tank. Some vehicles equipped with a rear window washer use a separate reservoir mounted in the rear of the vehicle. These rear reservoirs should be serviced in the same manner as the front washer reservoir.

Keeping a mixture of windshield solvent in the reservoir will help prevent freezing, but plain water will do the trick of keeping your windshield clean.

Buy fluid in the concentrated form rather than ready-mixed; it is cheaper and more convenient than lugging around gallon jugs.

For winter use in cold climates, use windshield washer solvent labeled for protection to 25 degrees below zero. Windshield washer solvent loses its resistance to freezing when exposed to heat, so the solvent labeled for 25 degrees below zero gives a greater margin of protection.

A tablespoon of dishwasher detergent added to each quart of the solution will help if dirt is a problem. If fluid will not squirt from the washer nozzles, check for an inoperative pump, broken or kinked hoses, a clogged filter screen in the tank (usually located at the end of a hose attached to the cap or inside the tank), or clogged nozzles.

Use a pin to unclog the nozzles that squirt onto the windshield.

Repairing Windshield Damage

A piece of gravel that strikes your windshield can cause a kind of breakage called bull's-eye damage. If it's small enough, or not directly in the driver's line of forward vision, the bull's-eye is often neglected. If one of the cracks extends to the plastic layer sandwiched in the middle of your windshield glass, moisture and ozone can enter, and the damage can slowly spread.

Traditionally, the only cure for bull's-eye or other windshield damage has been to replace the entire windshield. With the cost of that procedure escalating, especially for compound curved windshields, and with insurance companies more reluctant to pay for what can be considered cosmetic damage, another solution was obviously needed. Several manufacturers have devised methods to repair windshield damage. The most widely available, and one of the best of the repair kits, is sold through parts stores that cater to professional mechanics. It is furnished with a syringe containing a clear epoxy material, a mounting pedestal, and instructions. The repair cures in about half an hour and is waterproof. A careful do-it-yourselfer can handle this repair, though you may prefer to leave it to your regular mechanic.

Windshield Wipers

Normal use and exposure to the extremes of weather and will age wiper blades. Squeaks and jerky motions usually result from deteriorated blades. Depending on local conditions, a wiper blade may need replacement in as few as six months. In other areas they can last a year or more. Plan to replace your wiper blades annually if you regularly park outdoors.

What to do: Most wiper blades can be replaced in complete units of the rubber blade and its carrier. This method is the most convenient, but it is the most expensive. You can save considerable money by buying just the wiper blade insert, or refill, which is generally the part that wears out. This part is the rubber strip that actually wipes water from the windshield.

Inserts come in lengths of 12 to 18 inches, so measure your old ones to buy the right length. Pliers and gentle pressure can remove the old inserts, and you can usually install the new ones with only finger pressure.

To purchase an entire replacement wiper blade, you will need to know the year and model of your car, the length of the blade and how it is attached. Installation instructions are packed with the parts.

Windshield Wiper Interrupter

Many vehicles come from the factory equipped with windshield wiper interrupters, often called "delay." These slow down wiper action to as little as one swipe every twenty seconds for use. In a mist or light rain.

If your car did not come equipped with a windshield wiper interrupter, you can buy one for around fifteen dollars from a parts store. The kit will include specific instructions on how to install it. It might be a good idea to ask a counter representative to show you which wires to hook up and to suggest an appropriate location to mount the control under your dash. Be sure to position it where the driver's knee cannot accidentally come in contact with it.

One or more wires will have to pass through the firewall, separating the passenger compartment from the engine compartment. With a bright light, find one of the neoprene grommets through which other wires pass. There's probably room for one more wire, so you won't need to drill a new hole.

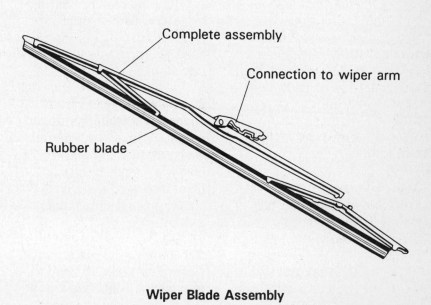

Complete assembly

Connection to wiper arm

Rubber blade

Wiper Blade Assembly

Replacing Your Windshield Wiper Motor

The windshield wiper motor, through linkages that are sometimes quite sophisticated, moves the wiper blades. Fortunately, the motor can almost always be replaced without involving the linkages. If you have a rear wiper, it will have a separate motor.

After many years of use, the motor can burn out. Before you attempt to repair it, be sure the motor is actually defective. A broken or loose positive wire, a blown fuse, a bad switch, a defective ground (negative) path, or a binding linkage can lead you to suspect the motor.

There are so many model variations that no single set of instructions can possibly apply to them all. A parts store should have a repair manual for your specific car, which will give you illustrated instructions. For a rear window motor, you may first have to remove a decorative cover or panel. Advice from the dealership or parts store may be helpful.

Repair rating: Adventuresome.

What you need: Tools vary from model to model, but you'll definitely need common and needle-nose pliers, different sizes of wrenches and sockets, a ratchet, and extension, and an assortment of screwdrivers (straight, Phillips, or perhaps Torx). Before starting, disconnect the negative cable from your battery.

An unscrupulous shop may replace a perfectly good motor and replace a blown fuse at no charge. Your wiper works again, but you've paid more than necessary. The only reliable test is to use the voltmeter portion of a volt-ohm-milliameter to find 12 volts DC at the positive terminal of the motor and then the ohmmeter section to find continuity to the ground from the negative terminal. Only after both of these tests can the motor be condemned. Even then, the linkage must be checked for binding.

What to do:
1. Buy the replacement motor, either new or used from an auto recycler. Having it at hand will help you understand the old one.

2. Remove the electrical connections from the broken motor. Usually, but not always, these are "polarized" so that you cannot re-install them incorrectly. In any event, make a simple diagram.

3. Remove the old motor. Generally, you will have to remove the connector that attaches the motor to the linkage and then remove the motor mounting bolts. These may be "shock mounted," which means the mounting bolts pass through soft neoprene washers. The same motor also drives the pump that serves the window washer, and sometimes the pump is removed with the motor and must be moved to the new motor.

4. With the linkage disconnected from the motor, check for binding. Binding occurs when a part of the linkage becomes worn, bent, or distorted in such a way that the mechanism doesn't move as freely as it was designed to move. It will take noticeable effort to move the linkage by hand, but this is your last chance to identify a linkage problem, which may coexist with and even cause a burned-out motor.

5. Replace the motor, pump, and linkage in reverse order. If the motor is shock mounted, be certain its grounding strap is replaced. This may be a heavy wire or a bare flexible copper strap that provides a path for the ground (negative) side of the electrical circuit.

6. Replace the electrical connections to the motor, referring to your diagram.

9

While the upkeep of your car's interior may not be what keeps it running, it does reflect the overall condition of the car. This chapter offers tips on how to clean, repair, and install the many extras in your automobile. These items include the upholstery, dashboard, door handles, rear-view mirror, and antenna. Our simple safety add-ons and suggestions will improve not only the condition of your car, but also the protection of its occupants. And, finally, information on theft prevention will help you to *keep* the car in which you've invested so much of your time, effort, and money.

In This Chapter...

Inside Repairs

Keeping it Clean

Safety Belts

Theft Prevention

The Rear-View Mirrors

What can go wrong: The glass portion of the mirror can break or the mounting can come loose.

Repair rating: Beyond Basic.

What you need: What you need varies greatly from one model to the next. Sometimes all you need is a tube of adhesive, a clean rag or paper towel, and a container of glass cleaner. Other models require small wrenches or tools.

Tip: An automotive recycler, or "wrecking yard," can be an excellent money-saving source for replacement mirrors and mirror assemblies.

What to do:

1. If only the glass is broken, see if you can buy the replacement glass a parts store. You'll find simple directions enclosed.

2. Many interior mirrors are attached to the windshield with a strong adhesive that rarely fails. You will find that this adhesive is an excellent product is easy to use and available at parts stores.

Tip: Often, the mirror assembly itself can be detached easily from its supporting arm. This makes the total job easier as it reduces the weight the adhesive must support while it is setting.

Radios and Stereos

The installation, replacement, and especially repair of automotive radio and stereo systems is highly specialized. Most auto repair shops, including most dealers, refer this kind of work to shops.

If you are replacing a broken radio or stereo, an auto recycler (junk yard) can furnish an exact replacement that you should be able to install. Having the replacement unit on hand will help to determine the location and method of attachment of the antenna, power leads, mounting brackets, and hardware.

Installing a sophisticated stereo system can be a time consuming and agonizing job. While none of the individual elements of the process are that complex, running the wires, removing the dash panel, and mounting the unit takes patience. Before considering doing the job yourself, find out how much the stereo shop that sold you the system will charge. If the price is high, then consider buying a system from a mail-order company called Crutchfield. They offer extensive telephone consulting, excellent instructions and all the extra parts you'll need to fit a stereo into your car. Call 1-800-336-5566 for a free installation guide and catalog.

High-Mounted Brake Lights

Starting in 1986, a federal law required all cars to have a high-mounted brake light as standard equipment. This additional brake indicator reduces the chances of rear-end collisions by more than half. If your car doesn't have this safety feature, you can easily add the stop lamp to your rear window. Note: Vehicles with roll-down rear windows, such as older station wagons, cannot add the high-mounted brake light.

There are two types of wiring systems for brake lights: a combined brake/turn signal (found on most U.S. manufactured cars) and separate brake wiring. To find out which system your car has, have someone operate the tail lamps while you stand behind the parked vehicle. With the left turn signal flashing, have him or her depress the brake pedal. If another bulb on the left side lights up and the turn signal continues to flash, you have a separate brake wiring system. The way to attach the wires depends on the system you have.

Repair rating: Basic.

What you need: You can purchase a high-mounted stop lamp kit at any parts store. It should include everything you need, with no special tools required. Make sure your kit meets SAE and FMVSS specifications.

What to do: The following are general instructions to attach a typical eye-level brake light, but make sure you follow the directions included with your add-on kit.

1. For the most secure attachment, first clean the inside of your rear window with window cleaner.

2. Measure the width of the rear window to find its center. Determine the correct placement of the light, but don't attach it until you've followed the wiring instructions.

3. Find the best route for the wiring. In most passenger cars, you can wire through the rear deck (you may need to drill a hole). For trucks, the wires go behind the seat, and they run into the door on most vans. Hatchback models may require you to remove the trim panels from the hatch and make a small hole for the wires to enter the car body. Follow the existing wiring, or catch the wiring with a stiff wire, such as a straightened coat hanger.

4. Once the wires are in the trunk, follow the kit's directions to connect the wires to your brake or brake/turn signal lamps and mount the light on the window.

To ensure the most efficient use of your brake light, make sure the light is properly angled. The brightest part of the light pattern should be at eye level of following vehicles, or 40 to 50 inches from the ground from 10 feet away.

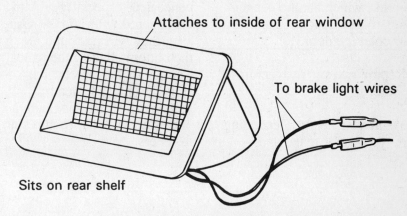

Attaches to inside of rear window

To brake light wires

Sits on rear shelf

Center High Mounted Brake Light

Replacing Door Handles

Broken door or window handles are not only unsightly, they can be dangerous. Handles on the inside of a door may be easily replaced by the owner. You may need only a Phillips-head screwdriver or an inexpensive tool called a window handle remover. Be sure you have the correct new replacement handles before you remove the broken ones.

Practically all handles on the outside of a door are removed and replaced from the inside. This involves removing the inner door panel on the inside of the front and rear doors. Many malfunctions of the inner workings of the door require that the door panel be removed in order to gain access for repair, replacement, or adjustment of parts.

What can go wrong: The door handle or latch may break, which can be dangerous if it no longer functions to open the door.

Repair rating: Adventuresome.

What you need: Depending on your car's make and model, you will need screwdrivers, a tool to remove door and window handles, a flat-bar, and a rubber mallet.

What to do:
1. Remove the armrest. It will be attached to the door by two or three sturdy screws that are angled upward into the door from the bottom of the armrest. The screws are usually Phillips or Torx.

2. Remove the inside door and window handles. Sometimes it is obvious that this can be done with a screwdriver. Depending on the make and model of your car, an inexpensive ($2) special tool may be required. Ask an auto body parts store representative about the specific tool required for your car.

3. Remove any screws that are holding the panel in place. These are sometimes partially concealed, especially in panels covered with fabric. Usually, they will be found along the bottom edge of the panel. The top of the panel often slips into place beneath a metal part of the door with a "pressure kit" that requires no fasteners.

4. Inspect the edges of the panel closely. Using your fingers only, gently pull it away from the door. Usually, it will be held in place by a friction pin. Carefully, insert the tip of the flat bar with one tine on each side of a friction pin. Cautiously pry the panel away from the door. Repeat this on each friction pin, until the panel pulls away completely. An adhesive sealer may hold the panel to the door, but pull with only moderate effort to avoid missing one fastener.

5. Inspect the new door handle to see how it is mounted. Then remove the old one and replace it. If the old handle is still good, a careful inspection will reveal the parts that need to be adjusted.

6. Replace all the parts in reverse order. Carefully position each friction pin directly above its proper hole in the door. Put each pin into place with the heel of your hand. When you're absolutely certain that each pin is lined up and properly started, tap the panel into place with the rubber mallet.

Your radio antenna collects broadcast signals, which are fed through a coaxial cable under the dash to the antenna input terminal of your car radio.

What can go wrong: A theft or an accident can cause the antenna to break at or above the mounting nut.

Repair rating: Basic.

What you need: A pair of slip-joint pliers with jaws sufficiently wide to loosen the mounting nut while the jaws of the pliers are parallel. One thickness of a shop rag should be placed between the pliers and the nut to prevent marring.

What to do:
1. Wrap the shop rag around the mounting nut, which is the plastic or metal device at the base of the antenna, holding it to the car. Loosen the mounting nut (turn counterclockwise) only enough so you can remove the "stub" of the old antenna, which extends downward for several inches.

2. Carefully remove the antenna and determine if there is a wire that can be disconnected just below the base. If so, carefully disconnect it, making sure the wire inside the hole doesn't slip down. If

not, you will need to disconnect the antenna from behind the radio and pull the wire out. *If you do this, tie a string to the radio end of the wire so you can pull the new wire back through the car.*

3. Take the antenna base with you to a parts store if you haven't already purchased the right antenna.

4. Install the replacement antenna. Check to be sure

it's mounted at the proper angle. The mounting nut is made in two or three pieces to allow adjustment of the angle, which is done by turning the bottom section a *small* amount.

5. Use the shop rag to re-tighten the mounting nut. Recheck the mounting angle. Pull gently on the newly installed antenna to be sure the mounting nut is holding it tightly.

Power Antenna

Some cars have "power antennas," and their replacement requires different tools and techniques from one make and model to the next. Replacement units are available new from the dealer or used from an automotive recycler. Follow instructions, and ask for advice at the parts counter. Replacing the entire power unit is an advanced job that involves disconnecting the antenna cable from behind the radio and the power wire, usually at the base of the unit. Both of these are under the dash and require a certain amount of body contortion to reach.

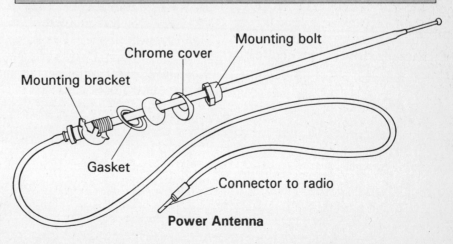

Power Antenna

Electric Windows

What can go wrong: A fuse can blow, a switch can fail, a power wire can break, or the motor moving the window can fail.

Repair rating: Adventuresome.

What you need: A volt-ohm-millammeter (v-o-m) is an essential tool. Otherwise, all you'll need is a few small hand tools. The replacement window motor can be found at a car dealer. You may want to check with an auto recycler, especially after you learn the price of a new motor.

What to do:
1. Before starting, check the fuse. Identify the proper fuse, using the diagram in your owner's manual. With the ignition switch on and the negative lead of the v-o-m connected to a reliable ground such as a metal part of the dash, check for 12 volts DC positive at both ends of the fuse. If battery positive is missing from either side, the fuse is bad. Replace it and test the window. For a more detailed description on checking and replacing fuses, see Chapter Six.

2. If the fuse is OK, test the switch. Often, you can access the bottom of the switch, where testing must be done, by removing only the switch panel from the armrest of the door. With a bright light, inspect it carefully to find Phillips or Torx screws, and carefully remove the panel. Look for a broken or disconnected wire leading into or away from the switch. If you find one, reconnect it and test the window.

3. With the ignition on and the black v-o-m lead grounded, check for 12 volts DC positive at both ends of the switch as you operate the switch through both of its positions. If positive voltage is missing from either side, the switch is bad and must be replaced with a new one. The new switch will come with its own directions.

4. Only if you complete the above tests without results, remove the door panel to access the motor. See instructions earlier in this chapter for how to remove your inside door panel.

5. Ground the negative v-o-m lead, turn on the ignition, and operate the window switch. You should find 12 volts DC positive at both "hot" terminals of the motor. If you do not, a wire is broken, possibly where it enters the door in a flexible conduit near a hinge. Patiently trace it and replace it. Sometimes you can pull through a new wire.

6. If battery-positive voltage is present at the motor's hot terminals, turn off the ignition and check for a good ground at the motor's negative terminal. If it is absent, install an alternate ground, turn on the ignition, and operate the window switch. If the motor doesn't move the window with battery-positive voltage to its hot terminal and a solid ground to its negative terminal, the motor is bad and needs to be replaced.

Dash Knobs

Knobs on the dash control such functions as headlights, windshield wipers, and radio volume.

What can go wrong: Knobs can be lost or loose.

Repair rating: Basic.

What you need: Usually, just your hands will work, although you may need a screwdriver. An exact replacement knob is also needed.

What to do:
1. Buy a replacement knob from a dealer or auto recycler.

2. Inspect the replacement to see if it is secured to the shaft with a set screw or if a friction device holds it. A typical friction device is a small piece of spring steel.

3. Slip the new knob onto the shaft. Rotate it to tighten the set screw, if there is one.

Adding Gauges

Dash-panel warning lights for engine temperature, oil pressure, and alternator condition are often slandered as being mere "idiot lights." However, warning lights offer an advantage that gauges do not: when they light up, they alert a driver to an abnormal condition.

Gauges, on the other hand, provide a more precise reading on exactly what is happening and often provide advance warning to avoid trouble. This is especially true of a temperature gauge, which in the event of trouble will begin to climb toward the red zone many minutes before the overheated condition trips the warning light. That's why owners of many cars that are factory-equipped with "idiot lights" choose to install, or have their mechanics install, after-market gauges.

Every parts store offers a choice of matching gauges, with mounting plates that make them attractive and convenient to install. Since their installation requires cutting into several engine systems, the job is often for professionals only.

Cleaning the inside of your car rarely requires special cleaning products. In general, what you use in your home will work just as well on the inside of your car.

Upholstery: Most fabric upholstery can be cleaned with a solution of one part household ammonia and three parts water. The key to success is not to get the upholstery too wet. Cloth rags generally work better than sponges, and you should change cloths as you work.

Begin at the outside of the stain and work toward the center to prevent a ring from forming when you're finished. When the stain is clean, dry the area as quickly as possible. If a ring does show up, repeat the process.

For vinyl upholstery, all you need is soap (nonalkaline is best) and warm water, which works just as well as the special vinyl cleaning products on the market. Rinse surfaces well and wipe them dry, because soap can leave a film. If your vinyl is old and faded, consider using a vinyl reconditioner after cleaning it. This product is available in department, hardware, and parts stores.

Leather upholstery should be wiped with a damp cloth and then dried thoroughly with a dry cloth. Use extreme care when cleaning perforated leather; you don't want to let moisture permeate the leather. Saddle soap and water can be used to treat difficult stains. After cleaning with the saddle soap, rub the leather with a leather preservative. Never use fabric or vinyl cleaners on real leather.

Dashboard: Cleaning the crevice between the dash and the window can be nearly impossible. You see the bugs and debris, but you just can't get to them. If a whisk broom or the crevice tool on your vacuum won't work by themselves, try them while the defroster is on. If that doesn't work, consider buying a small aerosol can of air, sold by hardware and office supply stores. These cans come with straw-like nozzles that fit into almost every crevice in your car.

If you have a faded vinyl dash, vinyl reconditioner can restore the sheen.

A vinyl dash may become cracked and damaged from exposure to ultraviolet light or high compartment temperatures. Many auto upholstery shops can furnish molded replacement dashboard covers that fit perfectly, since they are manufactured for specific vehicle models. An auto recycler or wrecking yard might be able to install an identical dash in good condition at fairly low cost.

Moldings: In time, the rubber-like moldings around the doors and windows may become hard and brittle. These door and window moldings need to be tended to for other reasons than appearance. They seal out rain, snow, dust, cold, and road noise, and taking care of them is important to keep them flexible and functioning. Spraying silicone lubricant on your car's weather stripping will prevent it from cracking and drying out and will keep it looking new. You can buy this spray at an automotive repair shop.

Vinyl Repair: If the vinyl on your seat or dash gets ripped, you may want to try using a vinyl mending kit. However, it is important to note that if the original vinyl ripped because of high stress, these products will not stand up to equivalent stress. If the rip was due to an accidental tear, the repair kit may work well. On older cars, for which color match isn't a major problem, try using colored vinyl or rubberized tape.

If the tear is bad, consider buying a new seat rather than having the old one reupholstered. Look in the yellow pages under "used auto parts" and call the wrecking yards near you. They may have your exact seat in great condition.

Windows: Any home window cleaner works on the windows and windshield, including a do-it-yourself mild ammonia or vinegar solution (4 tablespoons of either to 1 quart of water). Use a clean, lint-free paper towel to get into the corners. To avoid streaking, don't wash windows in bright sunlight.

Headliner: When your car's headliner (the part you see when you're inside and look up) tears or looks shabby from stains, you can have an auto upholstery shop fabricate and install a replacement. A less expensive alternative may be to order a headliner from a car dealer. When it's delivered, shop around for an installation price. An auto body shop is likely to install the new headliner at lower cost than an auto upholstery shop.

Carpet: For worn carpeting, the traditional repair has been replacement carpet, which must be custom-cut, sewn, and installed by an auto upholsterer. Now available are complete molded replacements, that are fabricated on forms identical to your car's floor. You (or a repair shop) can remove the front seats, take out the old carpeting, and replace it with the new, one-piece, molded unit! You'll pay more for the carpet but less for the labor, so the price is competitive. The color and quality of these units are comparable to the original, and they will give your interior a "like new" feeling.

Tip: Floor mats extend the life of your carpeting. They are also easier to clean and cheaper to replace.

If your carpet needs cleaning, your home carpet cleaner should do the job. Before cleaning stubborn stains, give the carpet a good vacuuming. Tank-type home vacuums with a brush and crevice tool work better than the little hand-held car vacuums that plug into the lighter.

Help for Stains

Here are some tips for some typical stains:

o   For grease and tar, try a solvent-type cleaner, such as paint thinner.

o   White or gray stains on the carpet are most likely salt stains from driving during the snow season. To remove these stains, scrub the area with hot sudsy water. A wet/dry shop vacuum will help to remove excess water.

o   If a cigarette burns your carpet or a small stain is impossible to remove, you can hide the spot with a piece of carpet from underneath the seat. Carefully cut around the bad spot, and glue or sew the new piece in place.

o   To remove chewing gum, try hardening the gum with ice and scraping it off. Another strategy for nonfabric surfaces is to spread a teaspoon of peanut butter on the gum. Leave it for 15 minutes while the peanut oil loosens the gum. Then clean the oil residue with soap and water.

o   If someone gets sick in your car, first scrape the area, then sponge it with a cold, wet cloth. Next, wash with warm, soapy water. Finally, use baking soda and water (1 teaspoon of baking soda to 1 cup of water) to deodorize the area.

o   To remove blood, use a rag soaked with cold water. Rinse and squeeze the rag frequently. Then use household ammonia to finish the job.

o   Chocolate usually comes out with warm water and mild soapsuds, followed by light rubbing with cleaning fluid. Remove stains from nonchocolate candy with very hot water followed by a mild soap solution.

Tip: Before you use a new cleaning agent, test it on a part of the carpet or upholstery that is hidden from view. Never use laundry soaps or bleaches.

Have you ever wondered if your safety belt will actually hold you in the event of a crash? Your belt is designed to move freely while you are driving, enabling you to reach all of the dashboard controls and remain comfortable. In the event of an accident or sudden stop, your belt is designed to lock immediately and prevent your body from moving forward.

Today's vehicles have two types of locking systems. Belt-sensitive systems lock in response to a sudden movement of the occupant's body, and the belt should catch when it starts to pull out quickly. If your safety belt locks in response to a sharp jerk on the belt, you have a belt-sensitive system.

If your belt doesn't grab when you pull on it, you probably have a vehicle-sensitive system. To test this type of belt, apply the brakes suddenly while driving (where it is safe to do so) and pull on the belt. It should lock up. If neither test results in the belt's catching, bring your car to the dealer and have the belts checked. You should also have your belts checked, and possibly replaced, if they have ever restrained you in a serious accident.

Tip: Avoid cleaning seat belts with bleach, which may weaken them. Regular soap and water is best. After you wash them, keep the belts pulled out so they can dry. If your belts won't automatically retract, take a few minutes to see if you can correct the problem. If not, get them repaired.

Rear Seat Safety: Lap and shoulder belts are currently mandatory in the rear seat of all passenger cars, but many models still on the road do not have this important safety feature. Since 1972, automakers have been required to provide anchor points for shoulder points in the rear seat, so a retrofit kit can be installed to provide adequate safety. Unfortunately, these kits may be difficult to find.

The Victim's Group Opposed to Unsafe Restraint Sytems (VIGOR) is promoting the replacement of lap-only seat belts with lap and shoulder belts. For more information, contact VIGOR, P.O. Box 375, Dunkirk, MD 20754, or call 213-866-6680.

Warning: Safety Belt Repair

Because seat belts are such a vital component of your cars safety system, it's generally not advised to repair them yourself. On the other hand, we have found that many dealers are resistant to repairing, replacing or adding lap and shoulder belts. If this is the case, we strongly suggest that you report the dealer's name and location to both the manufacturer (addresses are listed in the back of this book) and the U.S. Department of Transportation.

For years, safety belts have never had to meet crash-test standard, but the belt material itself has to meet certain standards. Make sure that any new belts installed or replaced in your car meet DOT standards. The belts will be so marked.

Preventing Theft

Keeping Your Car: A rapidly growing problem for car owners is theft. Car thefts are at an all-time high, and they will continue to increase as car prices go up and sophisticatedstereo and car phones become more common. But there is hope for car owners who realize that the most effective deterrent to car theft or break-in is into make it take time to get in your car.

Before you invest in an expensive and complicated anti-theft device, keep in mind that, according to the FBI most cars are stolen by "amateurs." About 80 percent of the cars stolen weren't locked, and 40 percent had the keys in the ignition. The basic idea is to make stealing your car a time-consuming prospect. If it takes a long time to get into, the thief will most likely give up and try his luck on someone else's car. That means that everything in your car that can be locked should be locked.

Inexpensive Theft Prevention: Here are some easy and inexpensive ways to protect your car from a thief:

1. Keep your windows tightly rolled up and always lock your car.

2. Never store spare keys in your car.

3. If you keep your car in your driveway, consider facing it toward the street. A thief will be less likely to raise the hood to hot-wire the engine if he or she can be seen from the street.

4. If you regularly park in lots where the attendants take your key, consider getting a different lock for your trunk. Don't tell an attendant how long you'll be gone unless you have to.

5. When you park on the street, turn your wheels toward the curb to make it more difficult for a thief to push your car away.

6. Replace the door-lock buttons with "anti-theft" buttons designed so that a coat hanger or wire cannot grab on to them. Just the presence of these types of knobs might discourage a thief from even trying.

7. Buy an alarm sticker (even if you don't have an alarm) and put it on one of your windows.

8. Contact your local police department and find out if they have a theft-prevention service. Many departments will provide a sticker and will mark key parts of the car and enter the number into their records. The purpose of these identifying marks is to deter the professional thief who is planning to take the car apart and sell the various components. Because the parts can be traced, your car becomes much less attractive.

9. On the top of the distributor is a short wire running to the coil. Removing the distributor wire is a rather inconvenient but effective method which makes it impossible to start the car. If you are leaving your car for a long time, you may want to try this. Don't forget to replace the wire when you want to get going again.

10. Locking gas caps are an inexpensive way to deter vandals from tampering with fuel supply.

11. If you have a hatchback, consider buying one of the window-shade devices that attaches to the top of the back seat, pulls across the back cargo area, and hooks onto the rear opening. This will enable you to hide packages in your cargo area. A cheaper way to accomplish the same objective is to carry an old blanket and cover your valuables when you park.

Specially Installed Anti-Theft Devices: Before you invest in an expensive anti-theft device, check with

126

your insurance company to see if installing the device will provide you with a discount on your insurance. The discount program (5 to 15 percent on your theft policy) is only available in a few states and the device may have to meet certain requirements to qualify. Following are several theft deterrent devices available to the car owner:

1.   A fuel shut-off valve will allow you to stop gas from getting to the engine, thereby keeping someone from driving very far with your car. These devices cost between $100 and $150 to install, and they allow you to open or close the gasoline line to the engine. One drawback is that the thief will be able to drive as far as a few blocks before he or she runs out of gas. If your car is missing, check your neighborhood first.

2.   Another way to deter the pro is to install a second ignition switch. In order to start your car, you will have to activate a hidden switch. Time is the thief's worst enemy and the longer it takes to start your car, the more likely it is that the thief will give up.

3.   The most common anti-theft devices on the market are alarms. The prices for

these systems usually begin at about $300 installed but can be several times more expensive depending on the level of sophistication. The complexity of the systems range from simply setting off your horn when someone opens your door to setting off elaborate sirens when someone merely bumps the car. These alarms are turned off and on by an exterior key-operated switch. Some people simply have the

switch mounted on their car and hope that its presence will intimidate the thief.

4.   A relatively simple, but not always effective, anti-theft device is called the "crook lock." It is a bar that locks the steering wheel to the brake pedal, making it impossible to steer or to use the brakes. "Crook locks" will deter sophisticated amateurs, but the pros can get them off.

Getting It Back

Here are some tips to help you get your car back if it is stolen:

1.   Mark your car in several hard-to-find spots on the engine and body, or drop a business card down the slot between the door and window. If your stolen car is recovered, these things will help to identify it.

2.   Don't keep your title or registration in the glove compartment unless your state law requires it. These documents make it easier for the thief to sell the car.

3.   Review your theft insurance policy. If you don't get your car back, your only recourse will be adequate theft insurance. Is your policy for full coverage, or is there a deductible? Does it cover items stolen from the car or stolen with it? In addition, does it provide for a rental car if your car is stolen?
   Insurance usually covers only the average value of your car when it was stolen. If you feel your car is worth more because of special equipment or unusually good condition, ask for Stated Amount Coverage. The extra cost may be worth it.

Locks

At some time, most drivers manage to lock themselves out of their car. If you have conventional door locks on the car, straighten out a wire coat hanger and bend the end into the shape of a hook. Insert it between the rubber molding and the window or vent window. Hook it carefully around the door button and pull it up.

If your car has the new, smooth, cylindrical buttons, the hanger strategy probably won't work. If the car is locked but the trunk is open, you may be able to move the rear seat and gain access to the passenger compartment.

Asking a locksmith to make a "car" call is expensive. Instead, find out your car-key code which may be on the key or may be available from the dealer or manufacturer. Every car key is coded by the manufacturer, and having a new key made is less expensive and aggravating than breaking a window or paying a locksmith. Keep the code number at home or in your wallet (unidentified, of course) so that you'll have it in the event of such an emergency. A locksmith can then make a key at the shop. You will have to show some type of identification to the locksmith, so hopefully your wallet wasn't locked in the car.

It's inexpensive to have spare keys made, and of course it's important to have a complete sets for the ignition, door, and gas cap. There are several types of containers at your favorite parts store for concealing keys, but make sure you can get at them from outside the car. Car thieves know all the good hiding places, such as inside a bumper, so it's a good idea to wrap the keys in reinforced strapping tape. It may take you a while to unwrap them, but it will also discourage a thief.

A new product makes carrying spare keys about as easy as it can get. This product is a set of metal keys that are mounted in a plastic card that resembles a credit card. The product is still in short supply and is only sold through professional locksmiths. With these keys, you can store a convenient set away in your wallet, and you're prepared for your next lock-out emergency.

A similar plastic product is sold through hardware stores, department stores, and key shops. Plastic seems like a good idea, but particles of the soft plastic wear off into the lock and cause problems. The plastic keys also break off and can be expensive to remove from the keyway. Stick with the metal keys that are sold by professional locksmiths.

Frozen Locks. When the weather dips below freezing, especially after a snowfall or freezing rain, drivers often discover that they can't unlock their car door because of a frozen lock. Calling a mechanic for road service may mean a long wait because the mechanic is likely to assign higher priority to other cold-weather emergencies.

First try the other doors on the car. Because of the wind direction or exposure of the car, only one side may be frozen. If that doesn't work, apply heat to the frozen lock. An open flame may damage your car's finish, but a hair dryer works well if you're near electricity. Another trick is to warm up the key in the flame of a match or cigarette lighter, and repeatedly insert it into the lock.

For prevention of future problems, shoot in a short amount of penetrating oil from a pressurized can. This will displace any moisture present and prevent the lock from freezing the next cold morning. At your parts store you may also find special lock lubricants that contain penetrating oil and powdered graphite which also work well.

10

Most of us have felt that sinking feeling in the pit of our stomach when our car makes an unusual sound or performs differently. The good news is that the problem is usually reparable.

This section will help you to "troubleshoot" those problems in order to get a head start on making the right repair. Remember that these are guidelines and not intended to diagnose every situation. They are based on extensive experience, however, and are quite likely to point you in the right direction.

Pay attention to what your car is telling you. Replacing a defective part promptly may save you a towing bill later on, and, more importantly, may prevent a serious accident. An automatic transmission that slips or stays in a low gear longer than it should probably got that way over a period of time. Taken care of immediately, it may need only minor work for around $40. Ignored for a few months, it may need to be rebuilt for several hundred dollars.

Immediate attention to seemingly minor problems usually saves you money and may save your life. This chapter provides a basic guide to what may be wrong when certain problems occur with your car.

In This Chapter...

Warning Lights and
   Electrical Accessories
Your Engine

Unfamiliar Noises
Additional Problems

What's wrong when your temperature light goes on or your temperature gauge is in the red zone:

This is a sign that your engine is overheating. If you are stuck in traffic and can't pull over, turn off the air conditioner and turn on your heater. Turning on the heat takes heat away from the engine. Next, if your car has a mechanical fan, put it in neutral and step on the gas. Getting the engine to run faster will make the fan spin faster. If the red light goes out after you take these steps, you can probably go back to using your air conditioner when you start moving again.

If you are not stuck in traffic, pull off the road, turn on your flashers, turn off the engine, and check the following:

1. You may have a leak in the radiator or one of the hoses. In either case, *wait for the engine to cool.* If the hose is leaking, tape it up. If the radiator is the problem, loosen the radiator cap one notch with a rag to relieve pressure, and drive slowly to the nearest service station.

2. You may be low on coolant. When the radiator is cool enough to touch, check the level of coolant by carefully opening the cap. The liquid should come up to the base of the cap. If it's low, add water with the engine running.

3. You may have a broken or loose drive belt. If so, wait until the car cools down some and then drive slowly until your warning light comes on again. Then stop and let the engine cool before starting up again.

4. Check the fan. If the fan is not spinning properly, it may cause overheating. An easy way to check, with the engine off, is to grab one blade and spin it. If the fan spins more than four or five times without stopping, the clutch is not working properly and needs to be replaced.

What's wrong when your oil light goes on:

If the warning light is working right, you've lost oil pressure and maybe oil, too. Pull off the road immediately, stop your engine, and check the oil dipstick first. If no level shows, don't drive until you've added some oil. If you have a spare quart of oil, put it in the engine, start up, and watch the warning light. If it doesn't go off within 30 seconds, stop the engine and call for help. I know of many instances where an ignored oil light led to thousands of dollars worth of engine work. Without oil, your engine parts get so hot that they expand and jam up. This can destroy the parts.

If your oil level shows full but the light stays on when the engine is running, don't drive any farther.

If the warning light just flickers when you're stopped in traffic, your engine may be idling too slowly or your oil may be getting thin or low.

Motor oil is the lifeblood of your car. Check it often, and don't go anywhere when you know you don't have enough.

Tip: Keep a quart of oil and a puncture-type can opener in the trunk for emergencies.

What's wrong when your brake light goes on:

With the parking brake set and the ignition on, the brake warning light will be illuminated. If the warning light goes on with the parking brake off, the ignition on, and the foot brake pedal depressed, pressure is low in one part of your brake system. Since 1968, all cars sold in America have two separate hydraulic systems that control the front and rear brakes. If one system fails, you should have enough braking power in your second system to stop the car. Test your brakes. If they still work, head slowly for a mechanic and avoid sudden stops. But if you suspect your brakes are not working, do not drive the car.

What's wrong when your amp or alternator light comes on:

If the alternator light comes on, do not turn off your engine. The light may have come on because your battery is not charging properly, so you may not be able to start the engine again. Keep driving until you can pull into a garage, service station, or somewhere where you can get a jump start. Keep an eye on the temperature and oil pressure gauges. The light might be on because of a loose drive belt.

What's wrong when your "Check Engine" light goes on:

If your "Check Engine" light goes on, your car's computer has detected trouble. When this light goes on, the computer system stores a specific code that indicates the problem. Either you, with the help of a shop manual, or your mechanic, should investigate the problem.

What's wrong when one of your electrical items fail:

If anything electrical fails--light, horn, radio--first check the fuse box. Fuses blow very easily, and you can replace them just as easily if you remember to keep a selection of fuses on hand. Your owner's manual has a diagram to show you what each fuse controls, and most fuse boxes print the purpose of each fuse somewhere near the box. If the same fuse repeatedly blows, you probably have a short circuit somewhere that needs to be corrected.

What's wrong when your heater won't work:

If the blower fan is not working, check the fuses. Perhaps there's a loose connection or a faulty switch. Usually fan motors give a warning before failing completely. Check your anti-freeze/coolant level. You may not be getting any heat because it is too low. If you have a temperature gauge on the instrument panel and it reads cool after you've driven for a while, have a mechanic check the thermostat. A thermostat that is not operating properly indicates that your engine may not be at its correct temperature. This prevents your heater from providing full heat.

What's wrong when your headlights don't seem bright enough:

They may simply be dirty. Wiping them with a damp cloth could clear up the problem.

If oncoming cars flash their lights when you have your low beams on, then you need to adjust your headlights.

It is possible to adjust some cars' headlights with a screwdriver and a specification manual. A mechanic, however, can do it in only five minutes with a headlight aimer.

What's wrong when your engine won't turn over:

If you turn the key, nothing happens, and all you hear is a click, the battery may be dead. First, however, check your headlights. If they go on and don't dim when you turn the key, the trouble may be with the neutral or park switch in your automatic transmission. Try jiggling the shifter in park or neutral while turning the key.

If the headlights don't work or if they dim when you try to start the engine, the problem is either a run-down battery or a poor battery connection. Loosen the battery cable bolts (remove the negative terminal first), pry the clamps apart with an insulated screwdriver, and lift the cables off. If this area is very dirty, follow the cleaning recommendations found in Chapter Six. If you can reach the contact where the ground wire connects to the chassis or engine block, check that also. Now, securing the grounded side last, reconnect everything tightly. Check the fluid level. (Don't smoke; explosive gases might ignite.) If the cells are low, refill them with distilled water. If the car still doesn't start, you may need to get a jump start and have your battery recharged at a gas station.

What's wrong when your engine turns over but won't start:

If the engine turns over but doesn't start and there's a strong gas smell, the engine is probably flooded. Check under the hood and make sure you don't see any gas. Wait a few minutes and then try cranking the engine for 30 seconds with the gas pedal pushed all the way to the floor. Don't pump it. If that doesn't work, open the hood and make sure your spark plug wires are attached to the engine. Give each one a push to ensure it is nested properly on the end of the plug.

If you haven't found the answer yet, your engine may not be getting enough air or gasoline. If there is gas in the tank, remove the top of the air cleaner and see if the choke valve is stuck open. If the engine is cold, push the valve shut and try to start the car. If that is not the problem, open the choke and look inside while someone pumps the gas pedal. If you can't see gas squirting, you've found the problem, and, unfortunately, you will probably

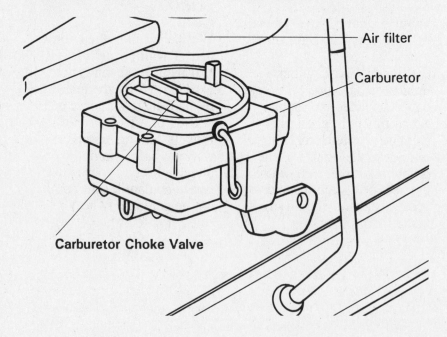

Carburetor Choke Valve

Air filter

Carburetor

have to get help. (This is one situation in which you should have a flashlight so you can look into those dark recesses.)

What's wrong when your engine sputters and spurts when idling:

A rough idle usually indicates that one of the cylinders is not working properly. In fact, if you have a large V-8 engine, you may drive for miles with one cylinder not working at all. Smaller, four-cylinder engines will run very roughly when one of the cylinders is not firing properly. In either case, you are wasting gas and could be damaging the cylinder. A rough idle usually requires an inexpensive repair, such as cleaning or adjusting the carburetor or injector jets or replacing the plugs and points.

Before you have any repairs made, however, open the hood and make sure your spark plug wires are securely connected to the spark plugs.

What's wrong when your engine dies while driving:

If you just splashed through high water, your ignition wires or distributor may be wet. Use a rag or paper towel to dry off the ignition

wiring. If the distributor cap is accessible in your car, dry that off, too--inside and out. Try to start the car again. If the engine still doesn't start, simply wait and try again after 20 to 30 minutes.

What's wrong when your engine knocks, pings, and sometimes won't shut off:

If your engine continues to run in a very jerky and unfamiliar way after you turn off the ignition or has a strange knock when you accelerate, you may be using gasoline with too low an octane rating. Experiment with higher-octane fuel before you take your car in for repairs.

What's wrong when your engine won't turn off:

If your engine continues to run off the ignition, it is after-running, or dieseling. After-running is not only extremely hard on the engine; it also indicates that something is out of adjustment. Perhaps the engine is running too richly; this reduces mileage and promotes carbon buildup inside cylinders. Perhaps the idle should have been lean-dropped and wasn't, which also lowers mileage. As a temporary measure, in an automatic transmission car,

stop the engine with the selector in gear. For a car with manual transmission, use the clutch to stop the engine. For a permanent cure, consult a professional. After-running, or dieseling, is too serious to ignore.

What you should do when a fire starts under the hood:

If you ever have a fire under the hood of your car, first turn off the engine and coast to an open area, away from buildings, other cars, and people. Turning off the engine turns off the fuel pump, so the fire will eventually burn itself out. Next, get yourself and everyone else out of the car, and get to a safe distance, at least a hundred feet away. Third, do *not* try to put out the fire! Call a fire department and wait for them to arrive. If you open the hood, you may provide a smoldering fire enough oxygen to produce a fireball. Besides, the hood release may be hot enough to cause third-degree burns on your hand. The fire department has asbestos gloves as well as training, experience, and equipment. Leave the fire to the firefighters and the repairs to your mechanic.

Unfamiliar Noises

What's wrong when you hear a strange noise:

The causes of unusual noises under your hood can be tricky to diagnose, and even trickier to correct.

The causes vary from simple to complex: a loose engine mount, dry or worn universal joints, worn gears inside the differential, bad front or rear-axle bearings, and even tires worn out of balance. As a do-it-yourselfer, you'll need a large supply of patience.

Different sources of noise respond in different ways, depending on whether you are driving, coasting, or floating. For the purposes of this kind of testing, "driving" means the car is accelerating under engine power. "Coasting" means your foot is off the gas pedal and the car is decelerating, either in or out of gear. "Floating" requires a light touch on the gas pedal, so you barely maintain speed on a level road. Determining when the noise occurs with respect to driving, coasting, or floating, and at what engine RPM it occurs, can help you to identify the source of the noise, which can then be confirmed by other testing.

1. A dull, nonmetallic thump from under the hood may indicate a loose engine mount. You'll notice the sound the instant you step on the gas pedal, or when you let off, at freeway speeds. Sometimes you'll notice the thump at low speeds. This is serious, so if you observe these symptoms, have your mechanic check out the engine mounts immediately. This problem could result in a runaway engine, which is when the driver loses control over the speed of the engine. It may be difficult to get the car under control, but that must be your first step. You can't count on brakes to stop a runaway engine, so put the transmission in neutral and coast to a safe place. Turning off the ignition switch may or may not stop the runaway engine. If it doesn't, lift the hood and yank out your coil-to-distributor wire. As a last resort, remove the air cleaner and stuff a large rag or towel into the top of the carburetor.

2. Most squeaks and rattles aren't serious. If you hear a new rattle, check for the following before you go to the service station:
o Loose screws and bolts (both inside the car and under the hood),
o Rear-view and side mirrors,
o Dashboard knobs and trim,
o Radio speaker grills,
o Window and door cranks and locks,
o Ashtray (is something inside? Has it been replaced tightly?),
o Glove box (is the door tight? Is anything in it rattling around?),
o Hub caps (check inside for pebbles),
o Outside trim.

3. Noises that are constant but slower than the engine speed, such as a "tick-tick-tick," usually indicate a serious engine problem.

4. A squealing sound can mean a loose drive belt. If the belt breaks, you'll hear a loud knocking sound. Don't drive with a broken belt.

5. A loud roar probably indicates a hole in the muffler. If the noise sounds as if it's coming from under the car, a mechanic can inspect the exhaust system for holes or loose fasteners.

6. Whistling or hissing indicates an air (vacuum) hose leak.

7. Wind squeals from closed windows may indicate that they are not closing fully and require adjustment by a mechanic. You may need new weather stripping.

8. Squealing brakes may mean the brakes need grease or new brake pads.

9. Squealing tires probably indicate that you need an alignment or that there is not enough air in them.

Additional Problems

What's wrong when you notice liquid leaking from your car:

Clear water from the air conditioner is no problem and is perfectly normal. Water that is brownish or green probably comes from your cooling system and should be investigated. If anything else is dripping, however, it could indicate a serious problem. For instance, red, pink, or light brownish greasy fluid indicates a leaky transmission. Black fluid indicates an oil leak. You might be able to locate a leak's source yourself very simply by cleaning the engine with one of the new engine-cleaning sprays, driving the car for a few miles, and then seeing where you have streaks of the liquid.

What's wrong when you smell something strange:

A burning odor could be caused by an electrical malfunction, an alternator problem, a loose hose, a belt trying to turn a jammed water pump, wiring trouble, a brake problem, or oil dripping onto a hot exhaust pipe.

Warning: The hydrogen gas from batteries can be explosive, so be careful.

If you smell gasoline, stop the car and look for gas leaking around the engine, fuel pump, and fuel line. If you see any, move away from the car. The hot engine could ignite the gasoline and cause an explosion.

The smell of burning oil may indicate that you're low on oil or transmission fluid. The smell of oil or exhaust in the passenger compartment might mean you have a faulty exhaust pipe.

A rotten-egg odor from the tailpipe area while the engine is running indicates that too much fuel is reaching the catalytic converter because of either faulty ignition or fuel problems.

What's wrong when you feel strange vibrations:

Unfamiliar vibrations can usually be felt throughout the car but most of the time through the steering wheel. They can be the result of fairly minor problems, such as a tire out of balance or some damage to the drive line. However, the causes can be extremely dangerous. If you notice unusual vibrations when you drive, beware: there may be a wheel bearing loosening, a driveshaft universal joint breaking, a transmission giving out, or a drive line part on the verge of failure. A damaged ball joint may be near failure, a wheel could fall off because of loose lug nuts, or the steering could fail due to a loose steering arm under the car. If the situation has developed suddenly, slow to about 10 to 15 miles per hour, put on your flashers, and proceed with caution to a nearby service station.

What you should do when your brakes are not working properly:

Never drive with defective brakes. If your brakes are sticking, consult a mechanic promptly. If you ever depress the brake pedal and your car won't stop, pump it quickly several times. If it still doesn't stop, use the parking brake. If you're making an emergency stop, apply the brake fully and quickly. This can cause your wheels to lock up, so be prepared for a skid. Otherwise, apply the brake gently and pull out of traffic as quickly as possible. Then have the car towed to a brake shop.

If your car doesn't have a brake warning light, be alert for increased pedal travel. If the pedal moves farther than usual, that's a symptom that fluid is low in the entire system or that one-half of the system has failed. Have your brakes checked at once by a certified professional.

What's wrong when your window leaks when it rains:

Make sure the rubber gasket around the top of the glass covers both sides of the glass when the window is closed. The rubber gasket may simply be out of place.

If that doesn't work, try putting 1/2-inch-wide black household weather stripping adhesive under the loose portions, or use a clear silicone sealer (it comes in a tube) to seal around the areas that are leaking.

What's wrong when your seat will not slide forward or backward:

First, look under the seat; something may be jamming the track. If your car is older, you may need to clean the tracks using a solvent and then spray them with a lubricant such as WD-40 (available in most parts and hardware stores).

What happens when you get stuck in snow:

However careful you may be, you will probably get stuck in snow sometime. If you get stuck, try to avoid spinning the wheels. A single rotation of the wheels may be enough to get the car out of the snow under its own power. Put the car in gear and press the accelerator very gently. If that doesn't work, try to "rock" your car out by taking your foot on and off the gas, but don't let the wheels spin for more than 10 or 15 seconds. When you rock the car, let off the gas the instant the car stops its forward rock. Turn off all accessories, and roll down the windows so you can listen to the wheels.

If you have front-wheel drive, turning the wheels to one side or the other will often provide enough traction to get the car out.

S-T-O-P, A-OK!

Here is a phrase to help you remember what to do when a dashboard warning light goes on: **S-T-O-P, A-OK**. This means "**S**top for **T**emperature or **O**il **P**ressure, **A**mps **OK**.

If your **A**mp or **A**lternator light is the one that comes on, there is a failure in your charging system. That merely means that your battery is not being recharged. Turn off all electrical equipment--except headlights if you need them--and you can safely drive to get help. Your car will run for up to an hour or two, but it's wise not to turn off the engine. Starting is a heavy drain on the battery. So it's *A-OK* to continue driving for awhile if the alternator light comes on.

On the other hand, if your oil pressure light comes on, immediately take your foot off the gas, coast to the nearest safe parking place, and turn off the ignition. You're probably just low on engine oil. If you have oil, put it in the engine, start up, and watch the warning light. If it does not go out within 30 seconds, stop the engine and call for help. Otherwise, drive slowly to a service station and top off your oil.

If your temperature light goes on, pull over safely, park, and turn off the engine. Wait for a full 15 minutes, cautiously remove your radiator cap, and pour in some water. If you cannot get any water, wait the full 15 minutes with the engine off and then drive the car toward help at a moderate speed, as long as the light stays off. If it comes back on, stop again for another 15 minutes of cooling. With luck, you should get a mile or more of driving for each 15 minutes of cooling.

An engine with no oil pressure or a bad cooling system can destroy itself in a matter of minutes. That's the *S-T-O-P* part.

11

When your car needs service, your first decision is whether to tackle the repair yourself or take the car to a mechanic.

While the purpose of this book is to help you do it yourself, finding a good mechanic is one of the more difficult jobs you'll face. Even as you become more confident and begin to tackle difficult repairs, a good mechanic is a must. And don't be surprised that your mechanic is willing to help. Good mechanics are proud of their knowledge, and they are usually willing to share it. In addition, your mechanic has test equipment which can help you diagnose tricky symptoms that signify simple repairs. You can also seek help from parts stores. They carry detailed guide books on particular makes of cars and on specific subjects, such as brakes, transmissions, engines, and much more.

If you do need to ask your mechanic for help, there are some common sense rules. You'll get more cooperation on a Tuesday when the shop is not too full than on a busy Saturday morning. If you need your mechanic's attention for a long period of time, offer to pay for the time; it will be money well spent.

Don't Fix It Yourself

While do-it-yourself repairs can save you money, some of the systems in your car are best left to an experienced mechanic's care.

Brakes: Every part of the brake system requires special equipment and precautions. Brake pads and shoes can contain asbestos, and working with this dangerous material requires special protection. Drums or rotors must be turned on a lathe to be certain they are true to shape and free of gouges. Wheel cylinders or calipers, as well as the master cylinder, must be either rebuilt or replaced. Even self-adjusting brakes need preliminary adjustment, and the hand brake, or parking brake, must be adjusted from under the car. Finally, the brake hydraulic lines must be bled to remove every trace of air, and they must be flushed to replace old, oxidized brake fluid.

Valve Adjustment: If you are skilled, experienced, and confident enough to remove your engine's valve cover and adjust the valves, you *must* have access to the exact shop manual for your specific car and engine. We do not recommend doing your own valve adjustments.

Sophisticated test equipment is required to determine whether adjustments have been made properly. Designs may become simpler, and thereby more conducive to do-it-yourself work. Until that time, shop around and have the adjustments made by a professional.

Air Conditioner: At the beginning of each summer, have your air conditioner checked out by a professional. Using thermometers and pressure gauges, he or she will check refrigerant and oil levels and catch problems while they're minor. During the winter, or any time you don't use the system regularly, turn it on for a full five minutes once a week. If at any time, winter or summer, the air conditioner does not blow cold air, have it checked out. A minor leak can cause expensive internal damage, especially to the compressor. The fee for this kind of routine maintenance is minor compared to the higher repair bills from not checking it.

Also, the systems presently in automobiles use a refrigerant called Freon. This gas has been associated with severe environmental damage. Federal law requires that its availability to the general public be severely restricted by January 1992 and elimi-

nated by 1993. Very soon, the only people who will be able to buy Freon will be certified air conditioning specialists who own Freon recovery equipment. Installing a one-pound can of Freon into a leaking system without first repairing the leak merely assures that another pound of Freon will leak into the atmosphere.

By the 1993 model year, it is expected that a new type of automotive air conditioner will use a newly developed and environmentally safe refrigerant, designated "R-134-A." Unfortunately, the two types of refrigerant will not be interchangeable.

Automatic Transmission: The workings of an automatic transmission are a mystery to most car owners, so the potential for ripoff is great. Some alarming symptoms, such as refusal to shift into high gear, can be caused by small malfunctions that can be repaired for a few dollars. On the other hand, seemingly minor symptoms, such as smoky brown transmission fluid, can indicate serious trouble. If you have any sort of problem with your automatic transmission, it's best to leave the diagnosis and repair to a professional.

Tip: Written Estimates

Always insist on a written estimate before you authorize work on your transmission. Getting this estimate is not as simple as getting an estimate for other maintenance and repair work, such as a tuneup. Finding out what's wrong will generally cost you first, and the shop should tell you exactly what the testing will cost.

If your transmission is ruined, you may need a rebuilt one. That would be the most costly job. Absolutely insist on being told the price, including installation. Make sure the shop gives you a written estimate covering the full price range of what it might cost.

If the mechanic will not give you these prices in writing, take your car to another shop, even if you have to tow it. Never allow a shop to work on your car if they tell you that they have to disassemble it before thay can give you a price. After the shop quotes its maximum price, you should ask for maximum estimates from two additional places. The difference can be hundreds of dollars.

How to Choose a Garage

Selecting a reliable repair shop involves two decisions. First, you have to decide what type of shop can best handle the work. One shop may specialize in exhaust systems, for example, while another may have an excellent reputation for fixing electrical problems. Second, after selecting the type of shop, you need to pick the individual shop and the mechanic that offer the best quality service and a fair price. Be certain that the shop you choose is familiar with your make and model car.

Here are some tips to help you choose a garage:

Call around. Don't choose a shop simply because it's nearby. Calling a few shops can save you up to 50 percent on a repair. A good rule is to eliminate the highest and lowest estimates; the mechanic with the highest estimate is probably charging too much, and the lowest may be cutting too many corners.

Check the shops's reputation. Before making a final decision, call your local consumer affairs agency and the Better Business Bureau to find out the shop's reputation. Remember, there are many shops they've never heard of and others on which they don't have sufficient records.

However, if their reports on a shop aren't favorable, you can immediately disqualify it.

Visit the shop. When you go to see a shop, look at the mechanic's environment, the shop, and the quality and condition of the equipment in it. This check is a good measure of a mechanic's potential, although not proof of knowledge. A clean shop reflects clean work habits, but does not necessarily mean that your car will get fixed properly.

Don't be afraid to ask whether the shop has the right equipment to do the work you need. But beware, simply having fancy equipment doesn't mean the mechanic knows how to use it.

Look for certified mechanics. A "certified" mechanic has passed the appropriate tests on car repair.

The National Institute for Automotive Service Excellence (ASE) operates a voluntary mechanic certification program. Certification can be earned in engine repair, automatic transmission/transaxle, manual drive train axles, front end, brakes, electrical systems, heating and air conditioning, engine performance, body repair, and painting and refinishing. A passing grade on the tests means that the mechanic is certified

for five years. After that, he or she must renew the certification with a new test in each area.

A shop can display the ASE sign, even if it employs just one mechanic certified in only one tested specialty. In addition, the certified technician may not necessarily be the one who works on your car. There is a greater probability of encountering this situation in a large shop.

AAA approved repair shops must offer a variety of services and sign a contract that specifies that the shop, when dealing with AAA members, must:

o Offer a written estimate that cannot be exceeded by over 10 percent without additional member authorization;

o Make available any replaced parts after repairs are completed, except parts that must be returned to the manufacturer to satisfy warranty claims;

o Guarantee its work for 90 days or 4,000 miles, whichever comes first; and

o Cooperate fully in any investigation of a complaint of an AAA member against the shop and abide by AAA's decision on the resolution of the complaint.

Kinds of Shops

The cost of a repair job, competently done, can differ greatly depending on if the shop is a new car dealer, an independent full-service shop, an independent specialty shop, a regional or national chain, or a franchised specialty shop. Each of these different kinds of shop offers you a mix of advantages and disadvantages.

Dealers: Dealers traditionally (but not always) charge the highest hourly shop rates, and their parts charges are invariably at full list price.

The dealer's service department is required to do warranty work. However, because they are reimbursed for this work by the manufacturer at a lower rate than they would charge you, they don't like warranty repairs. Incidentally, it is not true that periodic maintenance must be done by a dealer in order to keep your warranty valid. However, you are required to use a shop with certified technicians, and you must keep a record of all required periodic service. As cars and diagnostic equipment become more sophisticated, it is likely that more and more repairs will have to be done at the dealer.

Independent full-service shops: The independent full-service shop will also undertake work on most parts of your car. This type of full service is required for AAA approval. We often call an independent shop a garage or service station. While some of the finest mechanics can be found at independent stations, it's important to know who you are dealing with. Do not hesitate to ask for references, and use your intuition. If any type of shop will have a higher hourly rate than a dealership, it is likely to be an independent full-service shop.

Independent specialty shops: This type of shop works on only one system, or on sets of related systems. The brake-and-muffler shop is a common combination; both systems are under the car and require hoists. Tires and suspension (front end) are routinely paired at tire stores. By specializing in only a few tasks, this type of shop can keep a low parts inventory, and it does so much work in its specialized area that the mechanics learn to work very quickly. This efficiency can result in lower hourly rates and lower charges to customers. The downside is they may discover urgent work you need and not have the equipment or expertise to do it, which means another stop.

Regional or national chains: Most of the shops you consider national are actually franchised operations. However, a few exceptions are truly national. Firestone "Master Care" shops are all corporate stores; although there are independent Firestone stores, some of which provide other services. Prices normally fall between dealer and independent specialty charges. One advantage is that a warranty is valid anywhere the chain has an outlet. A drawback is that chains rarely do full-service work.

Franchised specialty shops: These shops offer many of the advantages of the independent specialty shop, including speed of service. However, they must generate as much profit as the independent shop to meet overhead and stay in business. Then, they must add additional profits to cover the franchise fee and group advertising. Also, some of them, but not all, engage in unfortunate high-pressure, deceptive sales practices.

Communicating With Your Mechanic

Communicating well with a mechanic is important to get the best results. The following hints will help you develop a friendly and effective relationship with your mechanic.

Show interest in the problem. Don't hesitate to ask for an explanation of what's wrong with your car. You'll be surprised at how helpful a mechanic becomes just knowing that you're interested.

Don't act like an expert. If you don't really understand what's wrong with your car, don't pretend that you do. It may only demonstrate your ignorance, setting you up to be taken by a dishonest mechanic.

Express your satisfaction. If you're happy with the work, compliment the mechanic and ask for him or her the next time you come in. You'll get to know each other, and the mechanic will get to know your car.

Let the mechanic diagnose the symptoms. Don't tell him or her what you think is wrong, because you might be wrong yourself. Tell the mechanic the symptoms, especially what the car is (or isn't) doing that made you bring it in. Let him or her determine the cause.

A good mechanic is a good diagnostician and should be able to tell you in simple terms what is wrong with your car.

Tell the mechanic what happens. Be specific. Does it happen all the time? Does it get worse or better under certain circumstances? Going fast or slow? While the engine is cold or hot? Did it start gradually or suddenly? Any unusual noises? With this information, and possibly a test drive, a good mechanic will have a better chance of pinpointing the ailment.

Be sensitive to your mechanic. It is much better if you have an appointment, and better yet if you can request work on a day in the middle of the week. Most people decide to bring their car in on Monday or Friday: Monday, because they had trouble on the weekend, and Friday because they would like it fixed in time for their days off. When a middle of the week appointment can be scheduled, the mechanic may have more time to do the job, and chances are you'll get better results. Arrange ahead of time just how long the shop will need the car, and try to allow as much time as possible not only to repair the car, but also to road test it to make sure the job was done properly. Do not stand over the mechanics's shoulder be-

cause you are in a hurry. Try to plan for some alternative means of transportation when the car is in the shop.

Get several estimates. Auto repair is a competitive business, and prices vary. You should also have each mechanic tell you what will be done for the price.

Be specific. If you sign a service order, make sure it has relatively specific instructions and a price estimate. Use the following steps to make sure the service order gets you the correct repairs and a fair price:

1. Be wary of blanket statements such as "fix brakes" or "repair engine." You could wind up with a complete brake job or new engine.

2. Never sign a blank order, and never tell the shop personnel to do everything necessary, unless the problem will clearly be covered by warranty. Instead, ask what exactly is being done and how much it will cost.

3. Have the shop call you if the work will exceed the estimate or if they are not sure how much work will be necessary.

4. Make sure you put your telephone number on the repair order.

5. Tell the service person that you would like to have any replaced parts when you return to pick up the car. Most good shops will comply with this, unless the parts must be returned to the manufacturer for warranty or sent to a specialist for rebuilding. However, you still have a right to see the parts before they are sent away.

6. Don't forget to have the person who writes the estimate sign it, and get a copy for yourself.

7. Check the estimate closely. Make sure each repair item is listed separately. If a tune-up is involved, be sure you know precisely what a "tune-up" includes.

Repair Rip-Offs

Beware of mechanics who find problems with your car that are not obvious to you while you are driving. They may tell you about worn shocks, unsafe tires, leaky radiators, misaligned front ends, or other parts that you ought to fix before they get worse. Take their advice, but first have someone you trust check it out. Do not give a stranger a big job.

The best protection against repair rip-offs while away from home is to have your car thoroughly checked before you leave. You should also have with you the tools and parts necessary to fix disabling but not serious problems, such as a broken fan belt, a flat tire, and blown fuses.

Here are a few of the dirty tricks of disreputable repair shops to watch out for:

o While checking under the hood, the attendant cuts the fan belt so that it hangs by a thread.

o A seltzer tablet is plunked into a battery cell, neutralizing some of the acid and causing it to boil over, which makes it look as if your battery needs work.

o The attendant doesn't push the dipstick all the way down when checking the oil and advises you that you need to add a quart.

o The attendant squirts oil on a shock absorber to make you think the seal is broken. Oil on your shocks does not really indicate a problem, whether it was squirted on intentionally or not.

o While checking the air pressure, the attendant punctures your tire with a sharp tool.

o The attendant may tell you that the oil filter is terribly hot and it needs replacing. Don't believe it.

Tune-Ups

Few terms in the car repair world are as misused as the term "tune-up." There are probably as many definitions for the word as there are mechanics who perform them. In addition, there are as many problems that a tune-up will supposedly correct as repair shops offering the service.

Because of extensive use of electronic controls, the old-fashioned engine tune-up that once entailed changing the breaker points, the spark plugs, and the distributor cap and setting the timing now consists mainly of changing the spark plugs, checking the timing, and replacing the air and gas filters.

Car companies generally recommend a tune-up every 30,000 miles, but hard driving may require one sooner. Many mechanics recommend a tune-up every 14,000 miles under normal conditions, and every 11,000 miles under severe conditions.

How do you know when your car needs a tune-up? You should always keep a running check on your fuel economy. First, find your average miles per gallon (check over three tankfuls). Then, if it drops by over 15 percent, you need a tune-up, and maybe some other work too. Other symptoms of an out-of-tune engine are: idling too fast when the car is warm, stalling, low power, rough idling, knocking or pinging, hard starting, misfiring, hesitation, black exhaust smoke, or if the engine continues to run when the key is turned off.

Remember, however, that these problems do not always require an expensive tune-up. For example, a common cause of problems is the idle speed: too low and the car can stall, too high and the engine continues to run after the key is off. A mechanic can adjust the idle speed quickly, with simple tools and a few dollars worth in parts.

Ignition timing is another cause of typical problems. It is often the reason for difficult starting, pinging under acceleration, or loss of power. Like idle speed, timing can be adjusted inexpensively.

Explain the symptoms and ask the mechanic to check the engine before replacing anything. If your engine is running well once some adjustments are made, forget major parts replacements. However, keep a constant check on the idle and ignition. A bad case of pinging can literally cause your engine to disintegrate over time.

A complete tune-up consists of at least five steps:

1. Checking cylinder compression to determine whether a simple mechanical problem exists.

2. Checking the full ignition and pollution systems against the specifications set down by the manufacturer.

3. Checking the idle speed, ignition timing, vacuum, mechanical advance, points dwell, plugs, condenser, distributor cap, rotor, ignition coil, spark-plug wires, and PCV system, with the proper equipment. The PCV, air filters, battery, automatic choke, and vacuum hoses can be checked visually.

4. Checking and changing all filters. They get dirty and can harm the engine.

5. Finally, a good mechanic will spray-clean the carburetor before adjusting it. There is no point in adjusting a dirty carburetor.

More than a third of tune-ups done today are performed by the car owners themselves. They may not do the whole process, but they can do most of it. With a few dollars worth of equipment and a shop manual, almost anyone who can handle a screwdriver, a pair of pliers, or any other common tool can do a tune-up. Why pay someone $40 or $50 to do something you could do in your backyard in a half hour with parts that cost about $15?

Saving Money On Repairs

Saving money on car repairs is not easy, but it is certainly possible. Here are five strategies to help you minimize your repair bills:

1. Develop a "sider." If you get to know a mechanic employed by a repair shop, don't be afraid to ask if he or she is available to work on the side, meaning evenings or weekends. The labor will be cheaper.

2. Use independent diagnostic centers. One of the major problems in getting repairs done for the lowest price is that a repair shop has a built in incentive to perform work that may not be necessary. If you suspect a major problem with your car, you should first take it to an independent diagnostic center. Since these facilities are not associated with repair shops, they have no reason to suggest repairs that are not really needed. The AAA runs many of these centers and the charge is usually $30 to $40. These diagnostic centers can also be useful for getting an unbiased opinion to settle a repair problem.

3. Double-up for service and savings. A fact that many motorists often overlook is that most car systems are interrelated. Servicing one system provides a good opportunity for servicing another. Knowing this will save you time and money!

o Whenever the wheels are removed, check (and service, if necessary) the brakes, front bearings, front suspension, the hand-brake, and the shocks.

o Whenever the starter is serviced, clean the connections and check the flywheel.

o Whenever the radiator is serviced, replace all worn hoses and the thermostat, change the fluid, flush the radiator, check the water pump, and perform a pressure test.

o Whenever the wheels are aligned, check the front suspension.

o Whenever the spark plugs are removed, check the compression.

o Whenever the distributor is opened, check the cap and rotor, and clean and lubricate them.

o Whenever the battery is serviced, clean the connections, add water, and check the hold-down bolt.

o Whenever the exhaust system is serviced, check the condition of the hangers.

o Whenever the dashboard is removed, lubricate the speedometer cable and silicone spray all wires.

o Whenever the car is on the hoist, check the frame, floor pan, and fluid lines for rust.

o Whenever the air conditioning is serviced, purge the system and replenish the refrigerant.

o Whenever the rocker cover is removed, adjust the lifters, if possible, and check the underside for varnish build-up, which indicates too few oil changes.

o Whenever body work is done, have new parts zinc-primed and painted.

o Whenever tires are changed, have the valves tested and the wheel rims balanced.

o Whenever the ignition wires are changed, change the cap as well.

o Whenever the intake manifold is removed, replace the lifters and change the gasket.

4. Use rebuilt and used parts. Buying a rebuilt part (one that matches the original specifications and has been totally overhauled) can save as much as 75 percent over the cost of a brand new part. When having repairs done, ask about rebuilt parts and the guarantee that comes with them. Used parts from a junk yard may be perfectly good, and they can cost one tenth of what a new part would cost.

5. Use vocational school and high school facilities. Contact your local school system and see if they accept cars for repair. Many times, your only cost will be parts, and the work is generally as good as you'll find anywhere.

Mechanics in an Emergency

There are thousands of honest shops who will help you out in an emergency at a fair price. There are an unscrupulous few, however, who will take advantage of your misfortune to rip you off. To protect yourself in an emergency, try not to be in a hurry. Accept the fact that you will be delayed, and don't compound the problem by allowing yourself to be cheated.

The corner service station you coasted into may be the most honest shop around. Here's how you tell. An honest mechanic will perform some tests to find out what's wrong. He or she may charge you for the tests but will tell you the charges beforehand. The mechanic will allow you to watch and will explain anything you don't understand. You can also expect a written diagnosis and a firm, written estimate with a guarantee that he or she will do the work proposed to solve your problem.

The honest shop won't mind if you ask to telephone your regular mechanic, read him or her the diagnosis and estimate, and ask if it sounds reasonable.

If the shop you're dealing with won't do these things, you may be in the hands of a ripoff artist. Even an expensive taxi ride to work and a bill to tow your car to your regular mechanic can be cheaper than a two or three hundred dollar scam. Remember: avoid urgency, and ask for testing, diagnosis, and an estimate.

Describing Your Car's Symptoms

Here is a list of questions from the AAA that will assist you in making helpful observations for the service technician:

1. How did you notice the problem?   Smell / See / Hear / Feel

2. Can you make the problem occur whenever you want so that you can demonstrate it to someone else?

3. Does the problem occur: Constantly / Intermittently
    Immediately after starting the engine or after____miles or____minutes?

4. Do any of the instrument panel gauges or warning lights react?
    Which instrument?   Which light?   What reaction?

5. What systems on the car are being operated when you notice the problem?
    Starter / Signals / Cruise control / Gear shift / Wiper washers / Air conditioning
    Clutch / Radio / Rear window defroster / Brakes / Heater / Other accessory

6. Does the problem occur when the engine is: Cold / Warming up / Hot / Over heated?

7. Does the problem:
    Change when *engine* speed changes and *car* speed remains same?
    Change when *car* speed changes and *engine* speed remains same?

8. What is the weather like when the problem occurs?
    All kinds of weather / Clear / Rainy / Snowy / Foggy
    Low humidity / High humidity
       Above _____ degrees F
       Below _____ degrees F
       Between _____ and _____ degrees F

9. Does the problem occur when the car is:
    Idling / Decelerating with brake / Accelerating / Maintaining constant speed
    Between speeds of _____ and _____
    At any speed / In gear
    Being shifted from _____ to _____ gear
    On rough road / On smooth road / Going uphill / On a level road / Turning a
    sharp corner / Going downhill / Taking a gentle curve / Pulling a trailer?

10. Where do the symptoms seem to be coming from in the car?
    Outside the passenger compartment / Right side / Left side / Front / Rear / Under
    the hood / In the trunk / Under the car / Inside the passenger compartment /
    Dashboard / Floor / Seat / Roof / Window

Resolving Repair Complaints

It's no surprise that auto repair complaints regularly top the list of complaint statistics. Each year we spend billions of dollars on car repairs, and few among us have not been victimized by a repair rip-off. While the statistics are overwhelming, knowing how to handle a repair complaint can tip the odds of resolving these inevitable problems in your favor.

The single most important step you can take for resolving problems in your favor is to keep accurate records. The following items are indispensible for speedy complaint resolution: service invoices, paid bills, letters written to the manufacturer or the repair facility owner, and written repair estimates from independent mechanics.

The following six key steps will help you to resolve your general repair problems:

1. Go back to the repair facility that did the work, and bring a written list of the problems. Be sure to keep a copy of the list. Let the repair shop have the opportunity to make good on a mistake. When you take the car back, speak directly to the service manager (not the service writer who wrote up your original order). Ask the manager to test drive the car with you so you can point out the problem.

2. Next, take the car to a mechanic you trust for an independent examination.

In many cities, AAA offers an independent diagnostic program for both members and non-members. Be prepared to pay $30 to $40 and get a written statement describing the problem and explaining how it may be fixed. Give your repair shop a copy. If your car is under warranty, do not allow any repair by an independent mechanic; you may not be able to receive reimbursement from the manufacturer.

3. If the repair shop does not respond to your independent assessment, present your problem to a complaint-handling panel. If the problem is with a new car dealer, or if you feel the manufacturer is responsible, check your owner's manual for an arbitration program. If the problem is solely with an independent dealer, your local Better Business Bureau (BBB) may mediate your complaint or offer an arbitration hearing. In any case, the BBB should enter your complaint into its files on that shop.

Tip: When contacting any complaint-handling program, determine how long it takes, who makes the final decision, whether you are bound by that decision, and whether the panel handles all problems or only warranty complaints.

4. If there are no mediation panels, you can contact private consumer groups or local government agencies. A phone call or letter from them may persuade a repair facility to take action. You can also call or write to your local "action line" newspaper columnist, editor, or radio or TV broadcaster. Send a copy of this letter to the repair shop.

5. Unfortunately, the next step is to bring suit against the dealer, manufacturer, or repair facility in small claims court. The fee for filing an action in such a court is usually small, and you can act as your own attorney, saving attorney's fees. A monetary limit on the amount you can claim varies from state to state. Your local consumer affairs office, state attorney general's office, or the clerk of the court can tell you how to file such a suit.

6. If you don't feel comfortable about going to small claims court yourself, select an attorney with experience handling automotive problems. If you don't know of one, the lawyer referral service listed in the telephone directory can provide names of attorneys for automobile problems. If you can't afford an attorney, contact your Legal Aid society.

Repair Protection By Credit Card

Paying auto repair bills by credit card can provide a much needed recourse if you are having problems with an auto mechanic. The Federal Trade Commission has provided the following example of a situation where paying by credit card could save the day.

Suppose you take your car to a mechanic because of a noise in the power steering. The shop does a rack-and-pinion overhaul. You pay $180 with your credit card and drive home. The next afternoon, the noise is back. Another mechanic finds that the real problem is fluid leaking from the power steering pump. That will cost another $125 to repair.

What happens if the first mechanic refuses to make good on the mistake? If you had paid with cash, you would be out $180 and might have to file suit to recover your money. If you paid by check, it would probably be too late to stop payment. Payment with a credit card not only gives you extra time, but it is also a tool for negotiating with the mechanic.

According to federal law, you have the right to withhold payment for sloppy or incorrect repairs. Of course, you may withhold no more than the amount of the repair in dispute.

In order to use this right, you must first try to work out the problem with the mechanic. Unless the credit card company owns the repair shop (this might be the case with gasoline credit cards used at gas stations), two other conditions must be met:

1. The repair shop must be in your home state (or within 100 miles of your current address), and

2. The cost of repairs must be over $50.

Until the problem is settled or resolved in court, the credit card company cannot charge you interest or penalties on the amount in dispute.

If you decide to take action, send a letter to the credit card company and a copy to the repair shop, explaining the details of the problem and what you want as settlement. Send the letter by certified mail with a return receipt requested.

Sometimes the credit card company or repair shop will attempt to put a bad mark on your credit record. You cannot be reported as delinquent if you have given the credit card company notice of your dispute. However, a creditor can report that you are disputing your bill, which can go in your record. The Fair Credit Reporting Act gives you the right to learn what information is in your file and to challenge any information that you feel is incorrect. You also have the right to add your side of the story to your file.

Using a credit card will certainly not solve all your auto repair problems, but it can be a handy ally. For more information about your credit rights, you can write to the Federal Trade Commission, Credit Practices Division, 601 Pennsylvania Avenue, NW, Washington, D.C. 20580.

Test Drive *Before* You Pay

Before you pay for a major repair, you should take the car for a test drive. The few extra minutes that you spend checking out the repair could save you a trip back to the mechanic.

If you find that the problem still exists, there will be no question that the repair wasn't completed properly. It is much more difficult to prove the repair wasn't correctly made after you've left the repair shop. It is legitimate for the shop to ask you to leave something of value while you test drive.

Warranty Repairs

Making your car last requires a good understanding of your warranty.

Every new car comes with two types of warranties: one provided by the manufacturer and one implied by law. Warranties provided by the manufacturer can be either *full* or *limited*. The best warranty you can get is a full warranty, which must meet the standards set by federal law under the Magnuson-Moss Warranty Act and must cover all aspects of the product's performance.

Any other guarantee is called a limited warranty. If the warranty is limited, it must be clearly marked as such, and you must be told exactly what the warranty covers. Most car manufacturers provide a limited warranty.

Any claims made by the salesperson are considered *express warranties*. Have these promises put in writing if you consider them important. If the car does not live up to promises made to you in the showroom, you may have a case against the seller.

The manufacturer can limit the amount of time that the limited warranty is in effect. In most states, the manufacturer can also limit the amount of time that the warranty implied by law is in effect.

Most automobile warranties have similar formats. The differences are usually in the length of time or the amount of mileage covered, how the powertrain is warranted, and how the car is warranted against rust. Your car also comes with an emission system warranty, required by federal law. Any repairs during the first five years or 50,000 miles will be paid for by the manufacturer, if an original engine part failure due to a defect in materials or workmanship causes your car to exceed federal emissions standards.

An increasing number of states are requiring an emission test before a car can pass inspection, so you may have to pay to fix the system if you have used the wrong type of fuel. Repairs to emission systems are usually very expensive, so use only the proper fuel for your car.

Finally, separate warranties are usually provided for the tires and the battery. Options, such as a stereo system, should have their own warranties as well, and the dealer provides service.

Most of us never read the warranty until it is too late. Since warranties are often difficult to read and understand, most of us don't really know what our warranties offer. Reviewing your warranty before repairs are needed can help later, by ensuring that you don't pay for covered repairs. Make sure you understand the fine points and the fine print.

Be careful not to confuse your warranty with a service contract. The service contract must be purchased separately; the warranty is yours at no extra cost when you buy the car. Service contracts are generally not a good idea, because the companies who sell the contracts are very sure that, on the average, your repairs will cost less than the price you pay for the contract. Otherwise, they wouldn't be in the business.

Warranty Warning

If you have not already done so, make sure that any "dealer-added" options do not void your warranty. For example, some consumers who have purchased cruise control as an option to be installed by the dealer have found that their warranty is void when they take the car in for engine repairs. If you are in doubt, contact the manufacturer before you authorize the installation of dealer supplied options. If the manufacturer says that adding the option will not void your warranty, get it in writing.

Warranty Complaints

If you have a problem that involves getting a factory-authorized dealership to repair your car under warranty, you can take the following steps:

1. Make sure you have a copy of the warranty available, and call the problem to the dealer's attention before the end of the warranty period.

2. After you have given the dealer a reasonable opportunity to repair your car, contact the manufacturer's representative (also called the zone representative) in your area. This person can authorize the dealer to make repairs or take other steps to resolve the dispute. Your dealer will have your zone representative's name and telephone number. Explain the problem and request a meeting and a personal inspection of your car.

3. If you can't get sufficient action from the zone representative, call or write to the manufacturer's customer relations department. Your owner's manual should have the phone number and address.

4. If these three steps don't bring action, present your problem to a complaint-handling panel or to the arbitration program in which the manufacturer of your car participates.

5. If you complain about a problem during the warranty period, you have a right to have the problem fixed even after the warranty runs out. If your warranty has not been honored, you may be able to "revoke acceptance," or return the car to the dealer. You may be entitled to a replacement car or to a full refund of the purchase price and reimbursement of legal fees under the Magnuson-Moss Warranty Act. Your state's Lemon Laws may also entitle you to a refund or replacement from the manufacturer.

Finally, you can contact the Center for Auto Safety, 2001 S St., NW, Washington, DC 20009. The Center can provide the names of lawyers in your area who handle automobile consumer problems. The Center also has published The Lemon Book, a detailed, 368-page guide to resolving automobile complaints. The book is available for $14.95 from the Center.

Using the Lemon Laws

A lemon is a car that just doesn't work properly. It may have one little problem after another, or just one big problem that never seems to get fixed. It has always been very difficult to obtain a refund if a car turns out be a lemon.

Because it is hard to define exactly what constitutes a lemon, it is difficult to win a case against a manufacturer. As a result of this problem, most states have passed "Lemon Laws," and the rest are considering them. Although each state has a different version of the law, there are some similarities: they establish a period of coverage, usually one year from delivery or the written warranty period, whichever is shorter; they may require some form of non-court arbitration; and, most importantly, they define a lemon. In most states, a lemon is defined as a new car, truck or van that has been taken back to the shop at least four times for the same repair or is out of service for a total of 30 days in one year.

If you need to use a Lemon Law, you must first determine if your state has one. Contact the Attorney General in care of your state capitol. If your state does have a Lemon Law, find out how it works.

12

You may want to contact one of the automobile companies to register a complaint, get more information about your car (possibly a copy of your owner's manual), or even send a compliment. Included in this chapter are names and business addresses of the top executives of each major automobile company doing business in the United States.

You can also use these addresses to write to the company with parts and service questions. Address your letter to "Parts and Service Operations."

This chapter also provides the names and addresses of some key government agencies that you can contact for assistance.

In This Chapter...
Automobile Manufacturers
Federal Government Agencies
Using the NHTSA Hotline
Vehicle Owner's Questionaire

Automobile Manufacturers

Mr. Karl H. Gerlinger
Chairman and President
BMW of North America, Inc.
300 Chestnut Ridge Road
Woodcliff Lake, NJ 07675

Mr. Lee A. Iacocca
Chairman and CEO
Chrysler Corporation
12000 Chrysler Drive
Highland Park, MI 48288

Mr. Sota "John" Fukunaka
President and CEO
Daihatsu America, Inc.
4422 Corporate Center Drive
Los Alamitos, CA 90720

Mr. Marik Bosia
President
Fiat Auto U.S.A., Inc.
777 Terrace Avenue
Hasbrouck Hgts, NJ 07604

Mr. Harold A. Poling
Chairman of the Board
Ford Motor Company
The American Road
Dearborn, MI 48121

Robert C. Stemple
Chairman of the Board
General Motors Corporation
General Motors Building
Detroit, MI 48202

Mr. K. Amemiya
President
American Honda Motor Co.
100 West Alondra Blvd.
Gardena, CA 90247

Mr. H.W. Baik
President
Hyundai Motor America
10550 Talbert Avenue
Fountain Valley, CA 92728

Mr. Kozo Sakaino
President
American Isuzu Motors, Inc.
P.O. Box 2480
City of Industry, CA 91746

Mr. Michael H. Dale
President
Jaguar Cars Inc.
555 MacArthur Blvd.
Mahwah, NJ 07430-2327

Mr. Yoji Toyama
President
Mazda (North America), Inc.
1444 McGaw Avenue
Irvine, CA 92714

Mr. Erich Krampe
President and CEO
Mercedes-Benz of N.A.
1 Mercedes Drive
Montvale, NJ 07645

Mr. Kazue Naganuma
President
Mitsubishi Motor Sales
6400 Katella
Cyress, CA 90630

Mr. Thomas Mignanelli
President and CEO
Nissan Motor Corp. U.S.A.
P.O. Box 191
Gardena, CA 90248-0191

Mr. Pascal Henault
President
Peugeot Motors of America
1 Peugeot Plaza
Lyndhurst, NJ 07071

Mr. Brian Bowler
President
Porsche Cars North America
One West Liberty Street
Reno, NV 89501

Mr. Robert J. Sinclair
President
Saab-Scania of America, Inc.
Saab Drive, P.O. Box 697
Orange, CT 06477

Mr. Graham Morris
President
Sterling Motor Cars
8300 N.W. 53rd St. # 200
Miami, FL 33166

Mr. Harvey Lamm
Chairman of the Board
Subaru of America, Inc.
P.O. Box 6000
Cherry Hill, NJ 08034-6000

Mr. Kenji Shimizu
President
American Suzuki Motor Corp.
3251 E. Imperial Hwy.
Brea, CA 92621-6722

Mr. Yukiyasu Togo
President and CEO
Toyota Motors Sales-USA
19001 S. Western Avenue
Torrance, CA 90509

Mr. Hans-Jorg Hungerland
President and CEO
Volkswagen of America, Inc.
888 West Big Beaver Road
Troy, MI 48007-3951

Mr. Albert R. Dowden
President and CEO
Volvo North America Corp.
Seven Volvo Drive
Rockleigh, NJ 07647

Mr. John Spiech
President and CEO
Yugo America, Inc.
120 Pleasant Avenue
Upper Saddle Riv, NJ 07458

Federal Government Agencies

Following are the federal agencies that conduct automobile-related programs. Listed with each agency is a description of the type of work it performs as well as the address and phone number for its headquarters in Washington, D.C.

National Highway Traffic Safety Administration
400 7th Street, SW
Washington, D.C. 20590
202-366-9550

Issues safety and fuel economy standards for new motor vehicles; investigates safety defects and enforces recalls of defective vehicles and equipment; conducts research and demonstration programs on vehicle safety, fuel economy, driver safety, and automobile inspection and repair; provides grants for state highway safety programs in areas such as police traffic services, driver education and licensing, emergency medical services, pedestrian safety, and alcohol abuse.

Environmental Protection Agency
401 M Street, SW
Washington, D.C. 20460
202-382-2090

Responsible for the control and abatement of air, noise, and toxic substance pollution. This enforcement includes setting and enforcing air and noise emission standards for motor vehicles and measuring the fuel economy in new vehicles.

Federal Trade Commission
Pennsylvania Ave. &
  6th Street, NW
Washington, D.C. 20580
202-326-2000

Regulates advertising and credit practices, marketing abuses, and professional services, and ensures that products are properly labeled (as in fuel economy ratings). The commission covers unfair or deceptive trade practices in motor vehicle sales and repairs, as well as in non-safety defects.

Federal Highway Administration
Highway Safety-HHSI
400 7th Street, SW,
  Room 3401
Washington, D.C. 20590
202-366-1153

Develops standards ensuring that highways are constructed to reduce the occurrence and severity of accidents.

Department of Justice Consumer Litigation Civil Division
Washington, D.C. 20530
202-724-6786

Enforces the federal law requiring manufacturers to label each new automobile and forbidding removal or alteration of such labels before delivery to the consumer. The label must contain the make, model, vehicle identification number, dealer's name, base suggested price, cost for all options installed by the manufacturer, and manufacturer's suggested retail price.

Identifying automobile safety defects is the responsibility of the U.S. Department of Transportation. Thousands of letters and calls are received by the department's National Highway Traffic Safety Administration (NHTSA) and are used as the basis of safety defect investigations. Often, those letters lead to recall campaigns.

NHTSA operates a toll-free Auto Safety Hotline. The Hotline operators can provide information on recalls, record safety problems, and refer you to the appropriate government experts on other automobile problems. For recall information, you need to tell the Hotline operator the make, model, and year of the car, or the type of equipment involved. You will receive any recall information that NHTSA has about that car or item. If you want a printed copy of the recall information, it will be mailed within twenty-four hours at no charge.

You can use the Hotline to report a safety problem. You will be mailed a questionnaire asking for information that the agency's technical staff will need to evaluate the problem. This information tells the government which vehicles are causing consumers the most problems.

Few government services have the potential to do so much for the consumer as NHTSA's database, so we encourage you to make your concerns known to the government. To make it as easy as possible, following is an actual copy of the Vehicle Owner's Questionnaire that you would receive from the Hotline.

You can either make a copy of the pages or remove them. When you've completed the questionnaire, simply fold and seal it with the postage paid address on the outside, and drop it in a mailbox.

After you fill out and return the questionnaire, the following things will happen:

1. A copy will go to NHTSA's safety defect investigators.

2. A copy will be sent to the manufacturer of the car or equipment, with a request for help in resolving the problem.

3. You will be notified that your questionnaire has been received.

You can also use this questionnaire to report defects in tires and child safety seats. Now that safety seats are required by law in all fifty states, numerous design and safety related problems have surfaced. If the government knows about these problems, hopefully they will take action so that modifications are made in these life saving devices.

For other car-related problems, the Hotline operators can refer you to the appropriate federal, state, and local government agencies. If you need information about federal safety standards and regulations, you will be referred to the appropriate experts.

You can call the Hotline day or night, seven days a week. If no operators are available, a recorded message will ask you to leave your name and address and a description of the information you are seeking. The appropriate materials will be mailed to you. Operators are available from 7:45 a.m. to 4:15 p.m. (Eastern time), Monday through Friday.

Free Safety Information

Auto Safety Hotline
800-424-9393
(in Washington, D.C.: 366-0123)
TTY for hearing impaired:
800-424-9153
(in Washington, D.C.: 755-8919)

Form Approved: O.M.B. No. 2127-0008

AUTO SAFETY HOTLINE

VEHICLE OWNER'S QUESTIONNAIRE

US Department of Transportation

National Highway Traffic Safety Administration

NATIONWIDE 1-800-424-9393
DC METRO AREA 366-0123

FOR AGENCY USE ONLY	
REFERENCE NO.	DATE RECEIVED

OWNER INFORMATION (TYPE OR PRINT)

LAST NAME	FIRST NAME & MIDDLE INITIAL	TELEPHONE NO. (Area Code) Work ( ) Home ( )

STREET ADDRESS	CITY	STATE	ZIP CODE

SIGNATURE OF OWNER	DATE

VEHICLE INFORMATION

VEHICLE IDENTIFICATION NO.*	VEHICLE MAKE & MODEL	MODEL YEAR

* LOCATED AT BOTTOM OF WINDSHIELD ON DRIVER'S SIDE

CURRENT ODOMETER READING	DATE PURCHASED _____ ☐ NEW ☐ USED	DEALER'S NAME, CITY, & STATE	ENGINE SIZE (CID/CC/L) _____ NO. CYLINDERS _____	☐ TURBO ☐ DIESEL ☐ GAS ☐ FUEL INJECTED

TRANSMISSION TYPE ☐ MANUAL ☐ AUTOMATIC ☐ 3 ☐ 4 ☐ 5 (Speed)	CRUISE CONTROL ☐ Yes ☐ No	POWER STEERING ☐ Yes ☐ No	POWER BRAKES ☐ Yes ☐ No	AIR CONDITIONED ☐ Yes ☐ No	BODY STYLE STAWAG _____ 4 DR _____ 2 DR _____ HATCH BK _____ VAN _____ PK UP TRK _____ OTHER _____

FAILED COMPONENT(S)/PART(S) INFORMATION (REPORT TIRE INFORMATION ON BACK)

COMPONENT/PART NAME(S)	LOCATION ☐ Left ☐ Right ☐ Front ☐ Rear	FAILED PART(S) ☐ ORIGINAL ☐ REPLACEMENT

NO. OF FAILURES	DATE(S) OF FAILURE(S) _____ MILEAGE(S) AT FAILURE(S) _____ VEHICLE SPEED AT FAILURE(S) _____	MANUFACTURER CONTACTED ☐ YES ☐ NO	NHTSA PREVIOUSLY CONTACTED ☐ YES ☐ NO

APPLICABLE ACCIDENT INFORMATION

ACCIDENT ☐ YES ☐ NO	FIRE ☐ YES ☐ NO	NUMBER PERSONS INJURED	NUMBER OF FATALITIES	PROPERTY DAMAGE (Est.) $	POLICE REPORT FILED ☐ YES ☐ NO

NARRATIVE DESCRIPTION OF FAILURE(S), ACCIDENT(S), INJURY(IES)

CONTINUE ON BACK IF NEEDED

HS-Form 350 (Rev. 11-86)

☆ U.S.G.P.O.: 1989-241-672/03360

Fold to show Return Address (no stamp needed) **Fasten with tape or staple and mail**

INFORMATION ON TIRE FAILURE(S) (IF APPLICABLE)

TIRE IDENTIFICATION NO.*

| D | O | T | | | | | | | | | | MANUFACTURER/TIRE NAME | SIZE |

* The identification number consists of 7 to 10 letters and numerals following the letters DOT. It is usually located near the rim flange on the side opposite the whitewall or on either side of a blackwall tire.

NARRATIVE DESCRIPTION (CONTINUED)

_____

_____

_____

_____

_____

_____

_____

_____

_____

_____

_____

_____

U.S. Department
of Transportation

**National Highway
Traffic Safety
Administration**

400 Seventh St., S.W.
Washington, D.C. 20590

Official Business
Penalty for Private Use $300

NO POSTAGE
NECESSARY
IF MAILED
IN THE
UNITED STATES

BUSINESS REPLY MAIL
FIRST CLASS PERMIT NO. 73173   WASHINGTON, D.C.

POSTAGE WILL BE PAID BY NATL HWY TRAFFIC SAFETY ADMIN.

U.S. Department of Transportation
National Highway Traffic Safety Administration
Auto Safety Hotline, NEF–11 HL
400 7th Street, SW
Washington, DC 20590

Index